MILLION DOLLAR MOM

No Sweepstakes Necessary to be a Stay-at-home Mom

Andrea English
and
Elaine Shepherd

Tate Publishing, LLC

"Million Dollar Mom" by Andrea English and Elaine Shepherd

Copyright © 2005 by Andrea English and Elaine Shepherd. All rights reserved.

Published in the United States of America

by Tate Publishing, LLC

127 East Trade Center Terrace

Mustang, OK 73064

(888) 361-9473

Book design copyright © 2005 by Tate Publishing, LLC. All rights reserved.

No part of this publication may be reproduced, stored in a retrieval system or transmitted in any way by any means, electronic, mechanical, photocopy, recording or otherwise without the prior permission of the author except as provided by USA copyright law.

ISBN: 1-59886-11-8-2

Dedication

This book is dedicated to all the mothers who long to discard their business suits or uniforms for the precious moments of full-time "mommyhood." The ache you feel in your heart is very real and we have written to tell you that you can choose another path. One that will remove this ache and replace it with a much different, yet distinct inner fulfillment. In the process we hope to change history one family at a time.

Acknowledgments

I would like to thank my wonderful family, Michael, Alex and William for their endless love and patience. To my mother, thank you for our brief but sweet fourteen years together. You gave me a lifetime of lessons on motherhood. And to my grandmothers, Annie Brown and Mable Earley for stepping in in the most superb way when my mother passed. I would also like to thank Dee Newnam for encouraging me every step of the way and Angela Kalo for diligently critiquing our manuscript. You both bring admirable respect to the role of being a stay-at-home mom. Last but not least, a special thanks to Elaine for being an awesome friend, fine Christian, and a splendid co-author.

Andrea English

I would like to thank my family. To my husband, Chris, for always letting me know how important you believe my job is and making it possible for me to fulfill that role. To my children, Leah,

Amber, and Tess for your love and surprises. I learn and grow from you each and every day. To my sister, Beth, you are so much more than my sister. And to my mom, Judy Zimmerman, who made me realize having children, being a stay-at-home mom, and teaching my children first-hand what I believe was the only career I wanted to pursue full-time. I love you all.

I would also like to thank Julie Bounds, Stephanie Mitchener, Amy Orman, Donna Pickering, Sheri Troxler, and Amy Zimmerman for their encouragement, support and prayers.

I couldn't possibly end without thanking Andrea. If it were not for you, none of this would have begun. Thank for starting me on a journey that has stretched me further than I could have imagined. I am so glad we have made this journey together.

Elaine Shepherd

Table of Contents

Preface 9
Introduction 11
Chapter 1   Our Stories 17
Chapter 2   First Things First 25
Chapter 3   Fixed Expenses & Lowering
            Household Expenses 31
Chapter 4   Credit Cards 39
Chapter 5   Groceries 45
Chapter 6   Meals & Meal Planning 59
Chapter 7   Eating Out 69
Chapter 8   Clothes 73
Chapter 9   Toys 81
Chapter 10 Yard Sales 87
Chapter 11 Birthday Parties 91
Chapter 12 Holidays 103
Chapter 13 Family Fun for Less 115

Chapter 14 Vacations 121
Chapter 15 Entertaining............... 127
Chapter 16 Babysitting............... 131
Chapter 17 Furniture & Decorating...... 135
Chapter 18 Miscellaneous 139
Chapter 19 When an Emergency Strikes... 143
Chapter 20 Priceless.................. 147
Conclusion........................ 151

Preface

Dear Readers,

There is a false notion today that you cannot afford to stay at home with your children and successfully live off one income. As rampant and widespread as this notion may be, it could not be further from the truth. This book is for those of you with hopes and dreams of one day staying at home. Hang on to those dreams as you ponder and cherish the words that lay ahead. May you realize that hope abounds you and dreams do still come true.

We have compiled a list of tips, tools and experiences for those of you who yearn to stay at home with your children. Our wish is that you will be able to utilize this information in order to make staying at home plausible for your family.

You will find we both share our individual thoughts and ideas about each subject discussed in a chapter. We specifically used this approach because we know that not everyone thinks the same way or fits into the same mold. It is our desire you will find aspects from both approaches useful as you aspire to stay at home.

Andrea and Elaine

Introduction

So you want to be a stay-at-home mom? You want to join the ranks of the growing number of women who are stepping out of the work force and into the domestic domain? Believe it or not, this is slowly beginning to happen. Census figures show that some 5.5 million, or 13 percent more women than ten years ago, are choosing to stay home. In the only recorded drop since 1976, the percentages of mothers in the work force from age 15 to 44 with children under the age of one, fell from 59 percent to 55 percent in the year 2002. But the stay-at-home mom is not a job for the weakhearted. It is a job that is grueling, exhausting, fast-paced, MAGNIFICENT and yet misunderstood in so many ways. But the most challenging things in life many times reap the greatest rewards. This aspiration is most assuredly one of them. Our aim is to educate you on how to make being a stay-at-home mom a reality, and how to make it work for your family.

First things first, what is keeping you from being a stay-at-home mom? Women report many reasons for being unable to make their dream become a reality. Examples include money, spousal disapproval, and love for their jobs. In order to move from thinking to acting, you must first identify your mind blocks and then deal with each individually. Let's take a good hard look at the top reasons.

Most of us will agree that money is the number one motivation to work. But how much money is enough money is a tough question. How much money we truly need is never as much as we think we may need. For most dual-income families, the bills are paid by both incomes. How do you cut your income and still pay your bills? We hope to assist you in this endeavor. However, we are not magicians. This process takes work. You have to want it. Once you have made up your mind that the almighty dollar is not going to keep you from your precious children, move to the Fixed Expenses section and get the facts on what you can do to make your dreams come true.

Before addressing the other obstacles for women not being able to stay at home with their children, let's see how much money you are really making at your current job. Does it really pay to work? Stop for a moment and look at how much it costs you to work. (Yes, I said costs.) Get out your calculator, pen, and paper and start adding it up.

MILLION DOLLAR MOM

- Daycare
- Taxes (Would you be paying less if just on your husband's salary?)
- Deductions for health care, dental, etc.
- Car Insurance (Insurance costs less when only used for "recreation")
- Additional gas money used to drive to daycare, work, and back
- Parking Fees
- Sick Days
- Work Clothes
- Meals on the go (lunches at work, dinners picked up on the way home instead of home-cooked ones)
- Donations to various funds at work (birthdays, flowers, gifts, etc.)
- House Cleaning (Do you pay for someone to clean your house since you don't have the time?)
- Are there any other conveniences that you pay for because you don't have time to do them?

This is not a complete list, just some of the larger ones. I challenge you to add them up and look at the total. After figuring up your real income, make sure to divide that by the time you are working (working hours plus driving time to and from the house). You may find that you are only making a couple of dollars an hour or less!

Another reason I hear when speaking to mothers is "my husband doesn't want me to." Now that's a tough one. You need his support, so how do you get it? Your best defense is to understand his reasons. Husbands report various reasons, such as, money, money, and money. Okay, that's not fair. Many may not be able to verbalize what they do not like about the idea; but for many they feel an overwhelming sense of financial responsibility to their family. Since he has had a financial partner thus far, it is frightening to him to imagine carrying the complete financial burden while lowering the family's overall income. I recommend beginning to decrease spending by utilizing the tips in the financial section of this book, then revisiting the issue when you have a track record to show your sincerity. Encourage him to read this book along with you.

Another issue that may make your husband uneasy about your new role may have nothing to do with money. It may have more to do with his childhood experiences. Maybe his mother was a stay-at-home mom and his father struggled with supporting the family. Maybe his mother was employed and he feels that he and his siblings turned out just fine. Each person's experiences will be different. Get your husband to talk about this topic openly and then share your childhood experiences. Gently express how important this matter is to you and keep communication open. You need him as an ally on this one. Good luck!

If you are one of the few women who absolutely loves her job, but still desires to stay home, you are going to have a difficult time making this decision. First, do you truly love your job or do you love the pay and/or the prestige that comes with it? These are difficult questions to answer because it is a package deal. Being a stay-at-home mom immediately deflates your net worth in a relationship, whether it is you or your spouse or both that feel this way. The redefining of the relationship can be difficult. The prestige of being a stay-at-home mom is nonexistent in this culture. You and your spouse have to esteem this position. Society will not do it for you. Ultimately, you have to be thick-skinned, confident and command the respect that you deserve in order to make this monumental life change successful. If none of this matters and you would still do your job even if you didn't get paid or no one respected the position, then you will have to prioritize which is more important to you. Unfortunately, life is full of difficult decisions. Decisions that require sacrificing or prioritizing. With societal pressure as it is, it will be difficult to choose your family. Elaine and I strongly believe that it is a decision worth merit. So keep reading and you will be able to see our intense love for this job and why we felt it so important to write this book.

CHAPTER 1
Our Stories

ANDREA'S STORY

Elaine and I decided to include our personal stories in our book. Well, I could go on and on about that subject. My wonderful husband Michael and I have been married 15 years. We have two precious and extremely rambunctious boys: Alex (eight) and William (five). Michael did not give me the liberty to discuss his annual earnings; however, I can share some general information. Since Michael is in sales, his monthly paycheck can vary dramatically. Put another way, it is either feast or famine, lobster or tuna. In order to make this variable one-income budget work, the monthly bills must be kept to a minimum. During times of feast, the extra money must be saved for emergencies or replenishing the savings account from previous emergencies. We have learned that in order for me to stay at home, we must separate needs from wants. All wants must be prioritized, but I am getting way ahead of myself.

How did I become a stay-at-home mom? For me this was and still is a gradual process. I was and still am career-oriented. I am a nurse by profession and although I do not love everything about nursing, I love being a nurse. When my first son, Alex, was born I scaled my hours back to part-time and placed him in part-time daycare. I learned quickly that this lifestyle was not for me. It went completely against my grain. I then rearranged my hours so that I worked several evenings a week and every other weekend. It was great for Alex but not so great for the marriage. Michael and I simply did not have time for each other. Although this was an exhausting schedule, being at home with my son made it all worthwhile. This schedule also maximized our earnings, since we were not paying daycare. I then weathered of this schedule and desired to stay at home. Michael, however, was not thrilled about the idea. Many intense conversations were had between the two of us. In order to show my sincerity I painfully trimmed the budget. Michael eventually joined the cause and we paid off every extraneous bill and minimized all others. Finally I was 100% at home.

When looking back to my childhood, I recall my mother in and out of work as a nurse and toying with a variety of schedules. I suppose her struggle became my struggle in later years, but she juggled all of them eloquently. We never discussed her inner struggles and she is not here to discuss it now. I have fond memories of all of our times, but my favorites were the ones when she was at home with us. If I had to do it over again, I think I would have done as many of my peers did and jumped in with both feet first.

ELAINE'S STORY

To understand much of who I am (my values, beliefs, convictions, and mentality toward family and finances) you don't need to look any further than my mom and dad. I am the product of a one-marriage, one-income, stay-at-home mom, Christian environment.

My mother stopped working outside the home when my oldest brother was born. From that day until the day she passed away 31 years later, she was a stay-at-home mom. She had seven children, the last of whom was born when she was 45 years old. Most couples might think that two incomes were necessary to help feed, clothe, and support all those children. Thankfully my parents did not think that way. They knew that my mom being home to raise their children, instilling their values and beliefs, was worth far more than some extra clothes and toys for each of us.

I bet you're thinking that my dad must have either had a great paying job or that we looked or felt deprived. Neither is true. My dad made a modest income and my parents stewarded their money in such a way that we never felt we were lacking. We lived in a home in a nice neighborhood and had everything we needed.

I will not tell you that living off one income is a piece of cake. It will be difficult at times and your friends and family might think you are crazy. This mentality and way of life is not the norm. Most couples feel like the goal in life is to acquire more things and give their children everything they never had. To do that, they need to work and work and work. As a result, they spend less and less time with their children.

My mentality is almost the exact opposite. I would rather give up unnecessary things—our children are worth it! I would rather spend time with my children than spend money on them and not be with them. Your children may not understand it all in the beginning, but each day you will be teaching them the most important things in life: They will learn that they are more valuable than things and money. They will learn the difference between needs and wants. They will learn to appreciate things and not take them for granted. They will learn the importance of others—the world does not revolve around them. They will learn the value of money and time management. They will learn how to be productive, contributing members of a household. They will learn that money does not bring happiness.

I could go on and on about the benefits your children will receive for living this way. I knew I wanted to be a mom, a stay-at-home mom. Yes, my children occasionally make me want to scream, they can drive me crazy and there are times Chris and I get frustrated financially. But do you know what makes all the difference in the world? Do you know what makes the hard days worth it? Stories like these . . .

We were in the process of building a house and things were going to be very tight to get in on Chris' income. We were going to move into the house a couple of days before Christmas and we told the kids (eight, six, and three years old) that the house was going to be our Christmas present. They would only receive one other gift on Christmas morning. Do you know what happened? There was no wailing and gnashing of teeth, no whining and complaining. Leah (eight) and Amber (almost six) said, "Okay, Mom." I was amazed, but cautious because I thought that when it came down to it, they would be asking for lots of things and be upset at the prospect of only receiving one gift.

Later, when we asked the girls to give us some ideas for their Christmas lists, they didn't want to name anything. Leah said, "Mom, I don't want you to buy anything for me. I want you to use the money for the house." After I picked myself up off the floor, I told her that the gesture was wonderful, but we would still like to have a list, both for us and for her grandparents and other relatives. She again insisted on not naming anything. It took 45 minutes of explanation and coaxing before we had a list. As if that wasn't enough, Leah and Amber got their heads together and decided they would have a yard sale to raise money for the house. They went through toys they weren't playing with, planned out a hot chocolate stand (it was fall) and drew pictures that they would sell to any "softie" that walked by.

Now please understand this is not necessarily my children's everyday behavior. There are days where they fight with each other, disobey, and can be selfish, but children are capable of so much when given the opportunity. When we plant the seeds of unselfishness, generosity, and sacrifice for something more important than their own desires, we will see them grow and blossom into beautiful, caring, giving people.

Just so you know the final outcome of this story—at Christmas, Leah never once complained about only receiving one gift. In fact, when people asked her what she received for Christmas she would tell them that the house was our big present, she got one other gift from mom and dad, and lots of presents from grandparents! Amber did ask as we opened gifts if there were any more. When we reminded her that the house was our present, she didn't whine, complain, or mention it again. Our three-year-old, Tess, didn't really notice anything at all.

If I had ever had doubts before about the value of my staying at home with the kids and giving up some of the extra things in life in order to teach them some of those important lessons, they would have been wiped away that day.

MILLION DOLLAR MOM

Why am I telling you all this? I was raised using much of the mentality that these tips and ideas entail. I know how it works and feels as a kid, and I know how it works and feels as a mom.

Just a couple more details about our family. Chris and I have been married 13 years. Chris' salary is less than $40,000. We drive two very used but reliable cars. We eat out some and go on the occasional vacation. We live in a nice neighborhood and have a mortgage. This information is given to you so you can see the things in this book work for real people. We are neither extravagant people nor do we deprive ourselves of all fun and joy. We are not a bunch of talk. We have to use these tips in order to survive as a one-income family. But as I said before, it's worth it!

CHAPTER 2
First Things First

ELAINE'S RECOMMENDATIONS:

Before we get into the specific details of how you can start saving money, I would like mention several things that I recommend you have once you begin this process. As you read further along in the book we will go more in-depth on subjects that will help you understand more why these things are so helpful.

My first recommendation is a week-long subscription to your local newspaper. I have found seven reasons why I believe a newspaper is well worth the cost of the subscription. If you use it correctly, you will be able to save hundreds or even thousands of dollars every year by just looking through the paper.

Reason #1 Weekly Coupon Inserts. You

would be amazed how much money you can save by taking ten minutes out of your day to cut coupons.

Reason #2 Weekly Grocery Store Ads. Our paper inserts the grocery store sale flyers in our Wednesday paper. If you do not get these flyers, you will not know what the stores' weekly specials and sales are, including the "Buy One Get One Free" items.

Reason #3 Notification of Double and Triple Coupon Sales. Occasionally, a grocery store (or drug store) will run an ad in the newspaper for a 3-day triple-coupon sale. Most of them will only double or triple a coupon for up to and including 50¢. You do need to watch the ads though, as every once in a while they will double or triple coupons up to and including $1. Those are the days where you get many things completely free!

Reason #4 Department Store Sales. Every week you will receive department store ads. Watch these for clearance, end of season, liquidation and going out of business sales.

Reason #5 Yard Sale/Moving Sale/Estate Sales. I cannot emphasize enough the value of yard sales. Typically, the prices at yard sales are between 10 - 25% of the retail price. Of course most of the items are used, but still . . . what a deal! You can find almost anything at yard sales if you go to enough of them and search them thoroughly: clothes, yard equipment, dishes and kitchen items, home decor, toys, books, furniture, sports equipment, tools, electronics. The list goes on and on.

Reason #6 Classified Ads. If you are looking for a larger, more specific item, check out the classifieds. Everyone thinks about cars, but you can uncover great deals on furniture, musical instruments, appliances, machinery, etc.

Personal Experience: My husband and I bought our first home and needed a sizable dining room table and chairs to fill a large area that served as our only eating space. My mom and I immediately started scanning the classifieds and found a beautiful table that included two leaves and eight chairs. Once the two leaves found their way into the table, we could seat 12 for dinner. The final negotiated price: $350. It is now more than 10 years later and that very table and chairs are still a permanent fixture in our home.

Reason #7 Notification on Community Events. The newspaper provides a convenient way to keep in touch with events occurring within your community. Typically, community events provide entertainment or recreation for free or at very reasonable prices for your family. Some community events that you can expect to see advertised in the paper are festivals, craft fairs, concerts, classes, holiday celebrations, and other special events.

As a final note about newspapers, would you like to cut down on the cost of the weekly subscription to the paper itself? (Did you really think that I would pay full price for it?) If you pay for six months or a year at a time, you can shave a little off the price. Slash the price of a subscription in half by joining in on it with a friend or neighbor. Keep your eyes open for a promotional deal. Once or twice a year our paper will run a promotional deal that gives you a gift card if you purchase a gift subscription for someone else. You buy one for your friend and she can buy one for you!

My second recommendation is a chest or upright freezer. A freezer can be a great way to help you take advantage of rare deals you find as you watch the grocery ads. Having a freezer can allow you to stock up on additional meats, cheeses, butter, breads, candy, frozen foods, etc. when there is a sale you just can't pass up. Not only that, but you can cook and freeze multiple dishes to use at a later date. Later in the book I will also include some general guidelines for how long certain foods can be stored in the freezer.

Recommendation number three is a coupon organizer. Once you start clipping coupons (and I hope you will) you will need a way to organize them; helping you utilize them the best possible way. Typically a coupon organizer can be bought for under $5. Just look for one that has many pockets so you can divide up your coupons in sensible categories.

Lastly you need a circle of friends as a support system. As Andrea stated earlier, society doesn't consider a stay-at-home mom as an important role. As a result there are times where you will feel discouraged/depressed. You have just made one of the most difficult but important decisions for your family. You are going to be adjusting to a different way of thinking and living. One of the best ways to help you is to be around other women who are in the same position. You will find that they will be a huge encouragement, great listeners, and an invaluable resource for new ideas. Your husband, as well meaning as he might be, will not always be able to understand some of the struggles you are going through. You need some other stay-at-home moms to talk to. You can also be a great encouragement to them. You will have a lot to offer other moms as you find the "tricks of the trade" that help you.

CHAPTER 3
Fixed Expenses & Lowering Household Expenses

FIXED EXPENSES - Andrea

This section is the most important aspect of this book. Proceed with extreme caution. "A tough pill to swallow" does not even begin to describe the lifestyle changes that are about to be proposed. Hang on tight—it's going to be a rough ride!

Let's start with the house payment. What percentage of your income is your house payment? If you bought your house based on what your lender told you you could afford, you probably overspent. Never allow any institution/individual that has an interest in your purchase to determine what you can afford. The bank and lending institutions have much to gain when you borrow money, and even more to gain when you default on a loan.

Their interest in you is strictly for their financial gain. Consider what Elizabeth Warren and Amelia Warren Tyagi have to say in their book *The Two Income Trap*.

> *In many cases, these lenders don't just want families' money; they also want to take people's homes. Banks have been caught deliberately issuing mortgages to families that could not afford them, with the ultimate aim of foreclosing on these homes. This practice is so common it has its own name in the industry: "Loan to Own." These lenders have found that foreclosing can be more profitable that just simply collecting a mortgage payment every month, because the property can then be resold for more than the outstanding loan amount. So the lender rakes in fees at closing and high monthly payments for a few years, then waits for the family to fall behind and sweeps in to take the property. The lender wins every possible way—high profits if the family manages to make all its payments, and high profits if the family does not.*

Keep your house payment at 25% or lower of your net monthly income. I realize this may mean a smaller house or an older house, but you are protecting your financial well-being. If you have already purchased your home, consider buying a less expensive home. This relocation does not necessarily mean a smaller home. You may need to move into the suburbs or in the county, or possibly purchase an older home. At any rate, the house payment must be lowered to 25% of your husband's net income.

Now let's consider the car payments—preferably the nonexistence of them. If you have two car payments, eliminate one by making a plan to pay it off as soon as possible or to sell it and purchase a used car outright. If you have one car payment, make a plan to pay it off early and then set aside money in your budget to get on a minimum of a ten-year car plan. In other words, drive your cars for a minimum of ten years. Better yet, drive it until it dies! Cars are a very poor investment. A new car loses value the minute it is driven off the lot. So if you do purchase a new car, utilize this information by purchasing a new car that is known for its quality and length of life and never intend to sell it. (I know, I know, you are probably not going to be a hot babe driving around in your old jalopy, but you are a mom now. Besides, you're not going to look that good with baby food stains on your shirt.)

Let's see—we have discussed the house and the car. Are you still with me? We're not finished yet. The power bill, water bill, phone bill, life insurance, car insurance, car payment, Internet and cable should take up approximately 10–20% of your net income. Keeping these bills below 20% will require some adjustments. Conserving on energy and water is not only good for the budget, but also good for the environment. It is also a great teaching tool when teaching your children to cut off lights and wait until there is a full load of laundry. In addition, cable and Internet must be evaluated according to the need. And, of course, shopping around for the best deals goes without saying. You will hear more about this in the Lowering your Household Bills section.

As Christians, Elaine and I can both attest to the blessings of cheerfully tithing a minimum of 10%. We have seen time and time again that when we give God our tithes first (before all other bills), He is faithful EVERY time to take care of us. So know that we believe it when we say that for Christians tithing must be a priority. Trust us on this one, your budget will not work without it. So just do it.

The remainder of your budget will be discussed in other areas of this book. I recognize that the percentages I have presented may have appeared scary when you converted them to actual dollar amounts, but this budget can work. If you made it this far and haven't thrown the book into the fireplace, you are doing great. Go fix yourself a cup of tea because you now have a set goal to work toward. You know what you need to do. You can do it! Elaine and I are in your corner and the following chapters will include many practical ways to help you make your budget work.

LOWERING HOUSEHOLD EXPENSES - Elaine

Insurance policies. Raise your deductible. You would be surprised the money you can save by raising that deductible. Call your insurance company (or several of them) and have them run the numbers for you. Another reason to raise your deductible is because more insurance companies are canceling policies after just one to three claims have been filed! A $500 claim is no longer worth filing if it means you could lose your policy.

Car Insurance. If you have a really old car that you are planning to drive until it dies, is it really worth it to keep collision/comprehensive? If it wouldn't be worth fixing after paying the deductible then consider just keeping liability. Also, don't forget about checking your deductible, and tell your insurance company that your vehicle is now for recreational use only. That should save you a couple of bucks too!

Heating/Cooling. Change your air filters every 90 days. This is the number one way you can ensure your system runs as effectively as it was made to run. Also make sure that your air returns are not blocked. If you are willing to learn to use it, get a programmable thermostat and set it to your advantage. Each night during the winter we set our heat to drop two degrees between 10 pm and 6 am. We are all sleeping snuggled under our blankets, our heating system runs less and we save money, yet we never notice the difference. Ahh, the beauty of the programmable thermostat. I bet you didn't realize you could save money in your sleep!

Water Heater. Make sure the thermostat on your water heater doesn't go above 120 degrees. That temperature should be hot enough for anything you need to do, not to mention that above 120 brings up the issue of scalding.

Water Conservation. While we are on the subject of water, if you are on city water, you are probably paying a lot for it. You can lower your water bill significantly if you replace old fixtures and appliances with new, more efficient ones. Purchase "low-flow" fixtures for your faucets and showers. Replace old toilets with the 1.8 gallon flush variety. Old dishwashers and washing machines can use up a lot of water. So when you need to replace any of these items, make sure they conserve your water.

Electricity. Replace regular light bulbs with fluorescent bulbs. Did you know that fluorescent bulbs only use 13 watts each? You can run four 13-watt bulbs for less than the amount of electricity it takes for one 60-watt bulb! Chris figured up the saving for us based on using thirty-five 60-watt bulbs for an average of three hours per day per bulb at our current rate of electricity. (I don't think we run each bulb an average of three hours and we certainly would have used several 100-watt bulbs instead of all 60-watt bulbs, but these numbers will give us the most conservative amount of savings for our house.) Most likely we save more than the below amount. Here's the outcome for a five-year period.

Thirty-five 60-watt bulbs $110
(Cost to buy and replace, life span 1000 hrs ea)
Cost of electricity/year ($184 x five yrs)........ $920
Total Cost over five years $1,030
35 Fluorescent bulbs $160
(Cost to buy, life span 8000 hours each)
Cost of electricity/year ($40 x five yrs) $200
Total Cost over five years................... $360
Total savings w/ fluorescent bulbs............ $670

 That is a savings of approximately $135 per year, not to mention the environmental and energy benefits!

 Cable/Satellite TV. Get rid of all the fancy/extra cable channels and go down to basic cable. You can save over quite a bit each month just by changing that one thing in the budget! Then use all that extra time that you are not spending watching TV and spend it with your children and your spouse, reading a good book, volunteering, or enjoying a hobby.

 Magazine subscriptions. Cancel them. Borrow them from your local library or ask people to give you those subscriptions for Christmas, birthday, or Mother's Day.

 Lawn Services. Unless there is some medical reason why you can't, get out there and do it yourself. In fact, if you get out there and sweat a little that means you might even be able to cancel your gym membership and save money there too!

CHAPTER 4
Credit Cards

CREDIT CARDS - Andrea

This section ought to be short for me. Credit cards? Get rid of them and quick! Use a debit card only that has a credit card capability for emergencies only. If you have any credit card debt, pay it off immediately using funds in your savings account. If you do not have a savings account, go on a financial diet ASAP. Do not pass go, do not collect $200 until you have paid off all credit card debt! This is serious business in my opinion. Debt may be the American way, but it will not secure your family's financial future. Good resources are any or all of Suze Orman's books and *The Millionaire Next Door*. In conclusion, ban credit cards from your home and read on about a financial diet.

CREDIT CARDS - Elaine

WARNING: The following tip can either make you hundreds of dollars every year or it can cost you thousands. Please read and consider it with extreme caution.

Credit card companies have long since been more than happy to take your family's hard-earned money with interest. They know that most people's eyes are bigger than their bank account and therefore they have enjoyed profiting from it. Well, it's time to turn the tables my friends, and the credit card companies are begging us to do it. There are now companies sending out applications for credit cards where they will pay you to use their card. You may not realize how to make money off the credit card companies, so let me enlighten you. This is the way it works. If you use their credit card, they will give you points or bonus bucks or something similar. After you have accrued a certain number of these items they will let you redeem them for specific rewards. These rewards may be anything from gift cards to airline miles to money off your credit card statement. Sounds great, right? *It is if you use it correctly.* You see, this program to reward you only truly makes you money if you pay your credit card off in full every single month. Ah ha! Therein lies the key. You must be able to be disciplined enough to use your credit card for all your necessary purchases without falling down that slippery slope of making purchases that you simply want but cannot afford. Once you start carrying a balance from month to month that piles on interest, you have easily lost the "reward" money plus some.

So, let me sum up here. If you have had problems with controlling your credit card purchases in the past, I agree with Andrea, don't use credit cards! If you can be disciplined with a credit card, be careful with it, but then enjoy every minute of spending the credit card company's money!

FINANCIAL DIET - Andrea

If you are asking what a financial diet is, let me explain. It is a temporary spending pattern that involves only necessities. It is not meant to be a permanent pattern of spending. It is strictly for the purpose of shedding extraneous debt. It can be done strictly or in moderation, depending on the desired outcome. In its harshest form it is spending money on necessities only. Items not permissible: eating out, clothing, movies, cable, manicure/pedicures, hobbies, haircare products (except for shampoo), hair treatments (such as color, perms, etc.), makeup, weekend entertainment, drink purchases, magazines. Are you getting the idea? Once you have lowered your spending to necessity items only, pay off all debt including credit cards, medical bills, appliances, vehicles, furniture and student loans. Then take the extra money and build up your savings account to *at least* three times your monthly income. Now you can slowly add your non-necessity items, starting with the most important. If an item requires using credit, don't buy it. You must spend in the present (cash) only. Otherwise, save up the money over the course of a few months and then purchase the item.

I realize that this type of diet may seem unbearable. You have to decide to what degree of this type of diet you can tolerate and for how long. Be realistic in your goals and then reevaluate as needed. Michael and I have done this twice in our lives: Once for a few months (in order to pay off credit cards) and once for approximately a year when I wanted to lower our income so I could stay at home. With regard to the latter, I kept every purchase to a bare minimum, paid off the credit card and several medical bills, the car, and saved money for any emergencies. I recommend the financial diet only for the purpose of paying off debt or adding to your savings or both. Once you have met this goal, you are well on your way to staying at home. The added bonus will be the security you have by living on today's income instead of tomorrow's.

CHAPTER 5

Groceries

GROCERIES - Andrea

I wish I could say I am a coupon person, but I am not. I've decided that there are two types of people: coupon-clipping people and non-coupon-clipping people. I fall into the latter category. My tips for grocery shopping are going to be fairly general. I utilize mainly generic brands. This no-name brand shopping saves me money consistently. There are times when a brand name item is within pennies of the cost of a generic, but usually it is at least 20¢ to $1 price different. I realize that some items are not as good, like ketchup. Don't be afraid to try an item. You can always go back to the name brand if you can't tolerate the taste.

Be aware that many of our favorite brands have begun lowering the quantity of food in the same package but labeling it with the same price. This type of marketing gives the company a raise unbeknownst to the customer. Always compare price to quantity.

I also recommend purchasing WIC approved items for two reasons. First, approved items are going to be cost-efficient, as that's how they become WIC approved. Secondly, the food items must meet certain nutritional requirements to be on the WIC approved list. (I learned this trick in nursing school during the public health resource study.) This technique is also time efficient: just scan the aisle for the WIC approved label. No lengthy time spent reading labels or comparing costs.

Grocery shopping starts with a grocery list, and a grocery list needs to start with a knowledge of what is already in the pantry. Rule number one, do not buy what you already have. Begin by going through the pantry and the refrigerator. Then, make a menu of meals by using items that you already have. Yes, you read that correctly, make out a menu of meals. I learned this tip from my friend Susan. I didn't think I could even do this, but I quickly realized that this tip had many benefits. It certainly answers that nagging question, "What are we eating tonight?" It also helped me see if we were getting a good variety of fruits and vegetables. And grocery shopping was greatly simplified by buying what was on the list.

Caution: This next section requires major lifestyle changes. Proceed with an open mind.

My next shopping tip to reduce the overall food cost is to forgo the junk food. When you look into your shopping cart do the cookies, chips and soda take up more room than the fruits, vegetables and milk? They shouldn't. You and your family can actually survive without any junk food. I know it is hard to believe and there may not be any living examples of this alive today, but survival is not linked to consuming junk food.

Switch your children's snack from half a bag of chips to half of a carrot. Cookies and sugary snacks should be limited to special occasions. In addition, get rid of all sodas and sugary drinks. Then, water down juice (half juice and half water) and limit juice to 4 oz. a day. Replace sugary drinks with water and milk (generic label only please, cows do not produce different types of milk for different manufacturers).

These tips will not only improve your budget needs, but also decrease your likelihood of obesity and improve your overall health. Would you use your hard-earned money to make you and your family overweight? Certainly not—at least not intentionally! Now I want you to take a sincere and honest look at the amount of food you and your family are consuming. I realize this is a tough assignment, but why pay to be overweight? Work on putting one half cup serving of two to three vegetables/fruit and a small serving of meat at each meal. Do not go back for more! Save leftovers for another meal. Watch your checking account increase and your waistline decrease. Now there's a change I can live with.

GROCERIES - Elaine

As you read this chapter you will be able to see why I believe a freezer and a network of friends are a vital part of saving time and money. Not only will you save more money if you have friends sharing in your same endeavors, but you will also have a network of people to encourage you.

You can regularly save 30–50% off your grocery bills (and occasionally save as much as 90%) by utilizing some of these ideas. Don't get me wrong, you will have to invest some time and energy, but if you do you will see the fruits of your labor. Using the following tips I am able to feed a family of six (my sister lives with us now) for approximately $300 - $325 per month. For that amount, we have all our regular meals, fresh fruits and veggies, some snacks and occasional desserts. That amount encompasses all of our household items such as paper products, cleaning supplies, napkins, and toiletries. We also include in that amount a small allowance for eating out or ordering in. Everyone needs a break occasionally and I enjoy a night now and then where I do not have to worry about cooking and conquering the inevitable mound of dishes bursting forth from the sink.

Okay, fasten your seatbelt . . .

Grocery Store Sale Flyers

By checking weekly grocery store flyers you will be able to find the sale prices at all the different stores and also find out when grocery stores are running Buy One Get One Free (BOGO) deals. Make sure you check the policies of the individual grocery store. Some stores charge full price for the first item and IF you purchase a second one it will be free. Other stores will charge half price for each one, so you really do not have to buy two items. If you do have to buy two items to get the deal, but do not really need both, see if a friend wants to split them with you. Also, Wal-Mart will match grocery store ads (except for BOGO). So even if you don't want to shop several different grocery stores, you can still save additional money by matching prices and using coupons at Wal-Mart.

Personal Experience: One week a local grocery store ad showed that they were having a sale on boneless pork loin. Regularly, the pork loin sold for $4.49/lb. The sale price was $1.88/lb. I bought one to slice into pork chops and another to cut into three roasts. Just by watching the weekly flyers I saved almost $30 on my pork loin purchase. That is nearly three month's worth of my newspaper subscription on that single item within one shopping trip!

A friend of mine was asking me for some grocery/coupon advice. I explained some of my shopping techniques and we picked up one ad from that particular week. We glanced at the front and back page of that ad. We found four items that she used which had great deals. We found her laundry detergent was BOGO ($6 savings), pull up diapers at $5.50 off regular price, $7 off with a coupon we found, chicken leg quarters at $0.17/pound, and two pounds of carrots for $1. Just by looking at those four items she regularly buys, she could save over $20. Now just imagine how much she could save if she looks through all the ads over one month's time!

Coupons

Coupons offer a fantastic opportunity to save money. Do not limit yourself to the one set of coupons located in your paper. Ask family and friends if you can use theirs once they are finished browsing through them. Another alternative is to ex-

change coupons with friends.

A couple friends and I used to get together once a week for a playgroup. At the playgroup some of us would bring our coupons. We began to notice the coupons that each other cut out regularly. One of my friends noticed I always cut out coupons for Wisk laundry detergent, but always left all the other laundry detergent coupons happily on their page. I knew Wisk detergent was a brand to which I did not have any allergic reactions, hence the reason for my selective snippings. One of my friends could use any brand of detergent, so she would always give me her Wisk coupons and she would keep other brands that she found coupons for. In turn, my friend's dog was very sick and required special (a.k.a. expensive) food. I knew that she needed those specific coupons, so I would always make sure my coupon made its way to her pile and I usually asked other people if I could have theirs in order that my friend could use them.

Do not just look for your "regular brands." Consider different brands as long as the coupons are worth using. My favorite coupons to clip are those that shave 75¢ off of a single item. These coupons are the most efficient for me because several stores in our area regularly double coupons up to 99¢. I can easily get 25%-75% off of the original price. The coupons go even further if the item I am buying is on sale that week. Check the grocery stores in your area to see what their policies are regarding coupons. Also, several times a year we will see triple coupon sales. Those are the times that you really can have fun and stock up.

Do not, however, be too picky when you are selecting coupons. A coupon for 50¢ off two is better than no coupon at all, and a 75¢ off can't always be doubled or tripled, but it is still a good coupon. You will want to familiarize yourself with the general prices in each grocery store chain. In many cases, an upscale chain will mean a slightly more expensive overall price, but if they offer double coupons up to 99¢ you will almost always save more money in the end.

When you are using your coupons, make sure to compare the prices to the store brand. Sometimes the store brand will still be a better deal than the brand name accompanied by a coupon. Also, do not dismiss the store brands too quickly. Some of them really are just as good and as tasty as the name brand.

Some coupon websites to check out are:
www.smartsource.com,
www.hotcoupons.com,
www.valupage.com.

But, my personal favorite and the one I highly recommend is *www.thecouponclippers.com*. Make sure to check it out!

Brand name vs. Store brand

I always buy Campbell's Tomato and Chicken Noodle soups (on sale with coupons, of course) because I prefer the taste of the Campbell's soups to the store brands. In contrast, if I can't get a good sale on the name brand "cream of" soups, I am happy to use store brands because I use them in casseroles. To me, the difference in flavor is lost when mixed with other ingredients.

I also know that sometimes the temptation is greater to buy the name brands because they offer reduced fat/reduced sugar/low carb versions or something else out of the ordinary. Make sure to check the store brands for those versions. Many of the stores now offer that variation in their brand.

Reduced for Quick Sale

Whenever you go in the grocery store, check for the "reduced for quick sale" items. Sometimes these items have been damaged slightly, discontinued, or are near their expiration date. You can get some incredible deals on items that are reduced for quick sale.

Damaged–the majority of the time items are discounted because the packaging has been dented or they have been returned. Okay, most people do not usually return food, but you might occasionally find a package of diapers that someone started to open and quickly realized that alas, it was the wrong size.

Discontinued/Closeout

These are items that the store is trying to get rid of because they have extra inventory, because the item is no longer going to be available to order, or the store has just decided not to carry it anymore. In order to make way for the new, more popular items, stores will discount the older, yet still quite usable items.

This is the area where they will place extra holiday/seasonal candy and decorations the day after the holiday has passed. This is an ideal time to stock up at 50% - 75% off. Did you know that you could store chocolate in the freezer for several years? You can! Just make sure that you store it in the freezer, not the refrigerator.

Personal Experience: After holidays I buy candy at 50% - 75% off. I leave the original package intact and put it inside a Ziploc bag and place it in my freezer. Many times the only part of the candy that denotes a particular holiday is the outside packaging. The individual wrappers are often not seasonal. So I can pull out some of that Halloween candy at Christmas and put it in my kids' Christmas stockings. I do the same thing with Easter and even for those last minute requests to send something in for a party.

Reduced for Quick Sale because of Expiration Date

Many times stores will reduce their meats and produce on the day before the "Sell by" date. Here is another opportune moment to save money without sacrificing quality. You can easily cook it that night for dinner, cook it and freeze it for another time, or freeze it raw and thaw it later when you are ready to use it for a meal.

Produce that is almost overripe–Here is the opportune moment to have fresh fruit that is kinder to your wallet. We all know that the most expensive way to eat is fresh fruits and vegetables (especially if they are out of season). Also, here lies the opportunity to do things like pick up those overripe bananas and produce some banana bread that you can give away to a teacher, pastor, new or sick neighbor.

Food Outlet Stores

Bakery Outlets–This delicious oasis can lend a helping hand in getting your breads for half-price or better. Most of the time these items are "day-old." If they are having a good sale, buy some extra and throw it in the freezer. Most bread keeps pretty well.

If you have not done it before, just buy one loaf to put in the freezer and try it after you have thawed it out. Some people really do not like it unless it is "fresh." I personally do not mind most of the time.

Check your area for other local food outlet stores. Many companies have these kinds of stores, for example, Pepperidge Farm, Sara Lee, Merita.

Farmer's Markets/Local Produce Stands– This is the place to get the freshest produce and it is usually lower than regular grocery store prices. Another plus—you are supporting your community by buying from the local farmers.

Warehouse Membership Stores

Warehouse stores can offer many bargain buys, but before you start buying in bulk be well aware of the cost of foods you wish to buy. You need to know (1) the regular costs of the foods you buy, (2) the average grocery store sale price and (3) the rock-bottom grocery store sale prices. When you are armed with this information you will be ready to attack the warehouse stores to see how they compare to grocery stores. Most people assume that the prices are better because they are sold in bulk, although, that is not always the case. Also you must remember that you cannot use coupons; you need a place to store it; you need to put it to use before it goes bad; you pay an annual fee. Make sure you can save the price of the fee many times over a year's time. If you have to travel to get there, you need to take that under consideration when you are trying to determine the amount of savings.

An excellent way to counteract some of the issues mentioned above is to group shop. Find two or three friends that like the idea of warehouse shopping. Make sure each of you are members of the warehouse club and determine some common items you all need. Then you can split up the items and the price. Instead of having to buy and store six 40-oz bottles of ketchup, you and your two friends each take two bottles and split the cost three ways. You don't need 177 bullion cubes? Split them with a friend and neither of you will have to buy them for a year! You can't eat five pounds of baby carrots? Again, split them with a friend. By using this method you do not have to store all of it, you pay a portion of the cost, and there is less of a chance for the food to go bad.

I didn't like warehouse stores at first. But then I went and took the time to check the prices. Once I did that, I knew which items were worthwhile. On the first shopping trip Chris and I made with our newly-bought warehouse membership card, we saved enough to cover the cost of the membership plus the gas to get there!

CHAPTER 6
Meals & Meal Planning

MEALS - Andrea

The nice thing about being a stay-at-home mom is that everything can be a challenge or a goal. You can actually make this fun: how can you be creative and cost-effective while providing nutritious meals? I am not a cook by nature. I come from a long line of great cooks, from my mother, grandmothers and aunts. And although I am a decent cook, I am certainly not an expert. My expertise is in lowering the bills, hence enabling survival on one income.

My basic advice is as follows:

Home-cooked food is cheaper than eat-out food. More importantly, it is healthier for you. Restaurant food is extremely high in fat, calories and sodium. You will be doing you and your family a great favor by preparing most of your meals at home.

Freezing and canning are great sources for containing food costs, as well as limiting sodium and reducing fat intake. They are also a wonderful learning experience for you and your child. If you don't know how, ask a friend to teach you or try www.homecanning.com.

Cooking in large amounts and then freezing in smaller portions for individual meals reduces many leftover items and simplifies later meals. A sealer can be extremely helpful in preventing freezer burn. I recommend a good sealer.

Instead of buying cookies, cakes or snacks for school/preschool/athletic teams, make them. If it is your turn to bring a snack for the soccer team, don't buy the individually pre-packaged items. Instead, buy a bag of vegetables/chips/cookies and separate in smaller portions in plastic wrap or generic brand snack baggies.

Use recipes from family members and friends, rather than cookbooks. These recipes tend to be more realistic, with regard to number of ingredients, as well as preparation time. I also recommend utilizing cookbooks compiled by church groups, schools, etc. These cookbooks are full of practical food that real people eat.

Serve water for adults and milk for children at meals. Serve water to children at snack time. Serve teas and colas at special occasions only.

FOOD PREPARATION AND STORAGE TIPS - Elaine

To help you conserve time and money, these

food preparation and storage tips will no doubt be useful. Here is where owning a freezer makes a world of difference.

When meats you eat hit rock bottom prices, buy as much of it as you can handle. Let me explain…I will use an example from earlier in the book. I bought boneless pork loin when it was on sale for $1.88/lb (reg. price $4.49). I had it sliced up in ½" thick slices and stored six bags with six slices of pork in each in the freezer. There were six meals for our family.

Now for ground beef I do something slightly different. I will usually buy 15–20 lbs of ground beef at a time should it by chance go on sale or is reduced because of a looming expiration date. I take it home, cook it all up, drain off the fat and then rinse it with hot water to get a little more of the fat off. By draining and rinsing, it significantly reduces the fat in the ground beef. After the meat has cooled I put about ¾ lb of cooked ground beef in sandwich sized Ziploc bags. I squeeze the air out of it, zip it shut, and press it flat. Then I put them in the freezer and let them freeze overnight. Once they are frozen solid, I get a shoe box and stack them up on end in the shoe box. The shoe boxes are a perfect size for storing and it keeps your food organized neatly in the freezer.

As for chicken, if I can get the flash-frozen, boneless, skinless chicken breasts on sale, I leave them as is and place them in the freezer. If I buy whole chicken or chicken quarters on sale I boil them, skin them, de-bone them, and let them cool. Once cool,

I divide them up into Ziploc bags, remove the air, zip them up and press them as flat as possible. Again, I place them in the freezer overnight and then put them on end in a shoe box. If you choose to, you can make chicken stock and freeze it for future use. Now obviously not all of your chicken dinners will use this same type of cooked chicken, but it will be perfect for casseroles, potpies, enchiladas, soups, and stews.

    Now when dealing with beef I either package it similar to the pork, or I have the meat department cut it into small stew pieces. For small stew pieces, I brown them, add onions and some spices, then add beef bouillon and water and let it simmer for several hours. After cooking for several hours, it becomes extremely tender and has an exquisite broth. I do not thicken the broth in any way at this time. I allow it to cool and divide up the meat and broth into Ziploc bags. (You know the routine—air out, stack flat in the freezer overnight and then place on edge in a shoe box.)

    When I want to use it, I thaw it out, heat it and then add things to the "base" to dress it up. (This is the time to thicken the gravy.) Here are a couple examples: For pepper steak, add sliced green peppers, some tomato sauce and serve it over rice. For chop suey, add chop suey vegetables and serve it over rice. For stew, add carrots, onions, celery, potatoes etc. For stroganoff, add sour cream and mushrooms and serve over noodles. The main thing to remember with the broth is that you do NOT thicken the gravy previous to freezing it.

Shredded cheese is another perfect item to freeze if you find a great sale. Small packages can simply be placed in the freezer. If you buy the 32 oz packages, just divide them into two-cup portions, put them in Ziploc bags and freeze them.

Deli meat can also be frozen. If there is a really good sale on deli meat, buy an extra pound or two and throw it in the freezer.

If you want to take your shopping a step further, mark your food with the date you bought it and the amount you bought. (On the packages of hamburger you might write 1 pound of 10 bought 2/10/05.) By doing this, you will get an idea of how much you go through in a given amount of time. This information will come in handy when you see a great sale. You will know that the 10 pounds of hamburger lasted you five weeks.

Cook and freeze one week to one month's worth of dinners in one day. Spend one day cooking. Freeze the dinners, and then pull them out when you are ready to use them. I especially like to make a large batch of meatballs, divide them up and freeze them for future meals.

Once you have done these things. You can start planning your meals for one, two or four weeks at a time. I find that two weeks is the most practical and efficient for me.

Meal Planning

Planning your meals out one to two weeks at a time is a guaranteed way to eat healthier and cheaper. Chris will be the first one to agree with this statement. I think the main reason is because I don't get stuck at 3:30 or 4:00 pm wondering what we will have or realize that I don't have all the ingredients to make a recipe. When I have those kinds of days, I usually want to ask Chris to bring something home or we eat hot dogs followed by a second course of macaroni and cheese.

I like planning out my meals because it typically means one trip to the grocery store. I am able to list and shop for all the ingredients I need for that one or two weeks' worth of meals. I stick to my list and it keeps me from impulsively buying things I don't need (most of the time at least). It also means a better variety to our meals. I can see our meals at a glance and be able to arrange them so we are not eating three hamburger dishes in a week and no chicken. When I was thinking about starting to plan my meals I worried that when Wednesday rolled around I wouldn't feel like eating chicken potpie. I soon realized that I didn't have to worry; I would just switch it for one of the other meals left that week. After all, I already had all the ingredients. The last reason I like meal planning is rather selfish. I ask my family for input on what meals they would like and mix their preferences in throughout the week. Do you realize what that means? I don't necessarily have to come up with every night's meal and I'm guaranteed to have smiling faces at the dinner table when the food is served because they have had a choice in the matter some of the time. Some of our family's favorite recipes have come from the *Taste of Home* magazines. My personal favorite is *Quick Cooking,* but *Taste of Home,* and *Light & Tasty* are also wonderful resources for finding recipes.

General Freezer Guidelines (Information from the test kitchens at Taste of Home)

The following times will give you an idea of when these food items will still be at their best. They are typically still quite usable and tasty beyond these time frames, but that all depends on how you store it, what kind of condition your freezer is in, and the temperature of the freezer.

Raw Meats

    Pork/lamb . . . . 4 to 6 mo.

    Beef (steak/roasts) . . . . 6 to 12 mo.

    Sausage. . . . . 1 to 2 mo.

    Processed Meats (Hot dogs,

    Bacon, Lunch meats, Ham) . 1 to 2 mo.

Raw Poultry

    Whole Chicken/Turkey. . . . . 1 year

    Whole Duck/Goose . . . . 1 year

    Chicken/Turkey Pieces . . . . 9 mo.

    Cooked meats/casseroles . . 4 to 6 mo.

Cheese

> Hard Cheese . . . . 6 mo.
>
> Soft Cheese . . . . 4 mo.
>
> Ice Cream . . . . 1 to 3 mo.
>
> Butter, Margarine . . . . 3 to 6 mo.

Have you ever considered a meal exchange? Arrange a get-together with several friends (let's say four) and exchange dinners. Agree on an approximate dollar value for each dinner so everyone spends about the same amount and make sure all the dinners can be frozen. At your first meeting, each woman should bring the recipe they are going to make. While you are there, make sure there is nothing to which anyone is allergic and make sure the costs of the meals are equal. After the recipes have been agreed upon, have everyone go back and cook five of the same dinner (one for you and one for each of your friends).

Make sure you cook the dinners in containers that can be labeled, frozen, and baked. Label each dinner with the name of the recipe, number of servings, date it was made, and cooking instructions. Don't forget to include a copy of the recipe so your friends can indulge in that meal any time they so desire. Exchange the meals and the next time you meet, give feedback on how each family liked the meals.

As you can see from my section, I don't have anything about gardening and canning. There is a reason for that. I can't grow anything to save my life! If you can, by all means do it because fresh food out of the garden and food you have canned is wonderful for you and your budget. Check out the resources Andrea recommended.

CHAPTER 7
Eating Out

EATING OUT FOR LESS - Andrea

When eating out, choose restaurants that allow children to eat free. A friend of mine compiled a list of restaurants that served free meals to children on assigned nights. This list was an invaluable resource.

Eat at expensive restaurants for lunch. My husband and I have a love for Thai, Japanese and Chinese food, all of which can be very costly. We would make a point to eat at these restaurants on his lunch hour. In addition, that was an easy time to get a friend to watch the children and then repay her the favor for her own lunch date.

I also recommend sharing meals with younger children or between siblings. Remember, this tip is equally important for the budget as well as for health reasons.

We reserve dessert eating for at home. We rarely order dessert in a restaurant.

I also agree with Elaine 100%; order water only in restaurants. It costs pennies for restaurants to serve tea and soda, turning profit on these items at approximately 98%.

A final note about eating out. Make sure it is a planned outing. By planning errands and activities that do not collide with meal times, you can prevent impulsive restaurant visits which can wreak havoc on the budget. Instead, make sure your restaurant visits will be enjoyable because you will know the visit is within your budget limits.

EATING OUT FOR LESS- Elaine

Scout out places where kids eat free and have everyone drink water. Most of us don't drink enough water anyway. You can save approximately $1.50 - $2 per person by not ordering a drink. For a family of four that's $6 - $8 right off the bat.

If you have younger children (under six) or children that don't eat a lot, many times you can share the food. Most restaurants serve massive portions of food. Many times Chris and I will either share a meal and get a second one with an extra side salad, or we will each order something that we will split amongst ourselves. Chris or I may order pork chops that come with a salad and baked potato. We can each eat one pork chop (they usually serve two), order an extra salad and then split the salad and potato with one of the kids. Spaghetti is an excellent shared dish. Most of the time they serve enough pasta to feed several people, so why not do just that? If you need more food, just order some extra garlic bread. It's usually cheaper than another meal.

If you are going to order a dessert, split it. At one particular restaurant we decided to really treat ourselves and order dessert. We knew that this restaurant's brownie sundae was enormous so we ordered one—with five spoons! Everyone was able to have ½ dozen bites or more, just enough to satisfy that craving for sweets.

Be creative and remember, most of the time you take food home. So this time try to order less and go home empty handed, but satisfied with both your appetite and your pocket book.

CHAPTER 8
Clothes

CLOTHES - Andrea

My husband laughed hysterically when I got to this section, as clothes and shopping just happen to be my weakness. That of course is hugely understated. Clothes and shopping are my Achilles heel—they are and will be my downfall. Even with this being as it is, I still have a few tricks up my newly-bought sleeve (ha ha!).

First, we love hand-me-downs. In this day and time, many folks are almost embarrassed by hand-me-downs. I've made it my personal mission to make hand-me-downs cool again. I sweeten the deal with my children by telling them who the previous owner was. This automatically increases the face value of the article of clothing. When friends ask if we would like hand-me-downs, we are always graciously appreciative. Too many times, we are throwing our money away for things that are simply not important to our children. Children care about how clothes feel, not look, and hand-me-downs always feel nice and soft. So in the future do not overlook this frugal resource.

If your children are older and becoming label conscious, give them a budget and allow them to decide how to spend it. Of course you will have the final say as to how the money is actually spent. The added bonus to this suggestion is that your child learns to budget and can appreciate the actual cost of clothing. (I must confess that I like the name brands too!)

Next, truly assess what your child's needs are. Children do not need a different outfit for every day of the season. Many times that is exactly what our children have. If your child's closet is so tight with hanging clothes that you can barely hang or remove an item, then your child has too much. If you or your child has unworn clothing that still has the tags on it, then you have too much. Scale back next season. I make it a goal to purchase no more than five pairs of shorts and shirts for a summer season, and two church outfits. Everything else must be a hand-me-down. This may sound slim, but my children have never run out of clothes. As a result their drawers are not so packed and they can easily put away their own clothes. My challenge to you is to trim the clothes budget next season.

In addition, outlet stores and consignment shops can be real savers. Not all items are a true deal, but these stores offer enough values to be worthy of exploration. On the flip side, be sure to consign your children's clothing, toys, and infant items. A friend of mine made $300 on one season of her child's clothing at a consignment shop.

My final trick is to buy at the end of the season. This technique allows me to get the shopping out of my system. I go after Father's Day and Christmas Day and purchase clothing for the next year. The sales price must be at least 50% off. My sister-in-law, Tracey, and I are insulted by sales prices in the 10- 40% range. These sales prices are for inexperienced shoppers. We want a real-deal, bargain-basement, something-to-brag-about price! Otherwise, the hunt did not result in a kill. So if you describe yourself as a "big shopper," try to limit your shopping to these times of the year.

CLOTHES - Elaine

First of all, I don't like shopping for clothes. I avoid it at all costs! I buy very basic (i.e. non-trendy) things that I can wear forever—less shopping for me. So, let's go over some basic tips on clothes. Not everyone may like this method, but if you are committed to staying at home with your kids, this provides a wonderful way to cut back on your clothes budget.

When you are buying clothes, buy the basics. Just like you have staple foods, you need to have staple clothes. I recommend basic colors for your pants, skirts, shorts, and capris: Black, khaki, navy blue, and denim. Almost any shirt you buy will match with several of these choices. Let your shirts, sweaters, and accessories add personality and color.

Do the same thing with your shoes—go with the basics that coordinate with most things. I'm not quite as strict with shirts, but I do always have basic black, navy blue, white, and red. Of course you don't want to buy plain everything, add color and prints that fit your personality. If you really look great in green, buy it in solids and prints. You can very easily wear green with all your basic color pants.

You can use this same approach with your kids' clothes. For the most part, keep their pants basic and let them have more freedom with tops. If you have girls that love to be girls, try to have them wear skirts or jumpers instead of dresses. A dress can only be worn one way, but a skirt or jumper can be worn with different shirts to change the look.

MILLION DOLLAR MOM

There are several places to find good deals on clothes. The first one is yard sales. We have done a majority of our children's clothes shopping at yard sales. We could not possibly afford to clothe three growing girls in brand new attire every season on Chris's income—not to mention the fact that I have a moral objection to paying that amount of money for clothes that don't actually come close to covering a decent portion of their bodies! (Oops, there's one of my soapbox issues. I better jump off quick!) There are many people out there who buy or are given *tons* of clothes for their kids. Those kids can't possibly wear all of them, so go to the yard sales and find some nice clothes at great prices.

Another place to find clothes for your children is at a consignment shop. I find them more financially beneficial for the 6X and up group. Most consignment shops are fairly particular about the condition of the clothes they sell, so you are less likely to find things that are stained or severely worn. Of course the way a consignment shop does business is that the original owner gets 50% of the purchase price and they get 50% of the purchase price. As a result, the prices are going to be higher than at yard sales.

Now even at consignment shops you can shop the sales and get better prices. Consignment shops don't like to keep extra clothes around so they will start to discount the merchandise if it hasn't sold quickly. At our shops they sell it full price for the first little while. But if it hasn't sold after a bit, they discount it 25%, after a little longer it's 50% off. If it is still there near the end of the season they will discount it 75% or have a dollar sale.

My kids are not particularly brand-aware, but if yours are department stores will have end of season sales to make room for new merchandise. They will usually run 50–75% off sales. By the way, have you noticed that many end-of-season sales start in the middle of the season? In December/January they are trying to get rid of all the winter items so they can start selling spring clothing in February. This is the time to buy for next year. This approach may not always work for kids because it can be hard to predict how they will grow over a year's time. But at the very least it is a great opportunity to buy for adults since most adults don't change drastically from year to year. My friend, Michelle, was telling me about how she buys for her boys. She shops the end-of-season sales and buys for the next year. She's been able to purchase name brand jeans for $6 or $7; London Fog coats (normally $140) for $20. Her mom shops the same way and one day was able to buy over $900 worth of clothes for approximately $140! That's my kind of shopping!

As of 2005, the following states participate in Tax-Free Weekends: Connecticut, Georgia, Iowa, Florida, Massachusetts, Missouri, North Carolina, South Carolina and Texas. During a designated weekend in each of these states the sales taxes on particular school-related items are waived. Items can include some clothing, school supplies, computer equipment, and select other items (varies by state). The discounts you acquire during these sales are not monumental, but they do offer a savings. Of course the stores always run sales during that weekend to bring you in, so you are likely to save more than 30–40%.

CHAPTER 9
Toys

TOYS - Andrea

Toys are the joys of our children's lives...or are they? Do your children have the latest and greatest toy on the market? Mine don't. This is an intentional situation on the part of my husband and myself. One of our concerns for children of this generation is the numbness obtained from a steady stream of acquiring items. Children cannot go to a restaurant, birthday party, or street festival without receiving something (whether it is a toy, a balloon, or another plastic cup to clutter my cupboards). Do you find yourself trying to purchase bigger, better or more expensive toys to impress your child? That is the numb reaction to which I am referring. In this case, less is better. Michael and I have tried to keep toy purchasing to birthdays and Christmas. No small goodies for behaving at the grocery store and no buying a toy just because everyone else in the class has one. When we give our children a toy, we want them to be wowed. We do not want to hear, "What else did you get me?" or, "Is that it?" By limiting toys to special occasions, children really do begin to appreciate what they have, as well as play with what they have. In addition, it is easier to clean and maintain their rooms. Now that is a huge bonus!

If you already have a large collection of toys, consider getting rid of some of them. Go through your toys and get rid of any duplicates. For instance, how many shape sorting toys do you need? Have a yard sale with the items and put that money away for Christmas or college. Remove any toys that you haven't seen your child play with in a while. Usually when I am removing toys, the children are not present. I know this sounds cruel, but my children will not part with anything. I then bag the items and place them in an obscure place. If after 30 days they have not missed the items, then the bag is cleared to be donated or sold. If you donate, be sure to save the receipt.

When purchasing toys, don't fall for the propaganda. No toy will make your child smarter. It is parental involvement in all activities that will improve your child's grades and success, not toys. Remember this fact when you are feeling compelled to purchase a toy for this reason.

When you are interested in purchasing a particular toy, don't fail to check thrift stores, consignment shops or to ask friends if they are willing to sell. Of course nowadays, eBay is an invaluable resource. I also save all toys for younger siblings. I store them in the attic then bring them out when they are age appropriate.

TOYS - Elaine

Most parents want to give their kids things that they want. Most parents also know that their kids don't *need* most of what they *want.* Kids really don't need that many toys. One of the things that reminded Chris and I of this was when we were building our house. We would go out to the land on weekends to work/clean, etc. Every time we went out there with the girls all they wanted to do was play in the sand and gravel piles. One Saturday we were out there for over five hours and only had to speak to them a few times (about getting along, not being bored). The entire time was spent in the sand and gravel. Another time we were out there for nine hours prepping and seeding the lawn. We built a fire to burn some extra tree limbs. I bought marshmallows and hot dogs. The kids had a ball roasting things over the fire, keeping the fire going (with parental supervision of course) and playing on the hay bales. I know it sounds insane, but the kids stayed happy and had fun. The outdoors seems to be the best toy that a child can have. For those times where the outdoors is not available, consider keeping more basic toys around the house. The following is my toy suggestion list. Remember to limit the number of these toys to a reasonable amount. Blocks/Lego bricks, bubbles, vehicles (cars, trains), boxes (i.e. Appliance), dolls/action figures, sport equipment (balls), art supplies (crayons, paint, play dough, etc.), computer games (we prefer educational), fake food (let them use your pots and pans).

Books are not included in the toys list because those are another entity all together. Kids should have plenty of books and they are easy and cheap. You can go to two weeks' worth of yard sales, or pick some up at a library sale and walk away with more than you can carry. Also, I would venture to guess that if you went to the library and borrowed 30 books each week you wouldn't read the same book twice for years.

Each of the items on the above list will foster

creativity, imagination or independent thinking in your child. They will help with everything from math to gross and fine motor skills. Think about it—how many times have you heard (or said to someone yourself) that a child had more fun with the box a toy came in than the toy itself. So, don't spend your hard-earned money on expensive toys that they will forget before the month is out.

Obviously there are toys that your individual children may really enjoy. For those items, here are some ways to get them cheaper. (1) Consignment shop. Most likely your kids won't even realize that it's used. (2) eBay. You can find virtually anything on there. Check it out to see if they have what you are looking for. Just be careful not to get caught up in the bidding and end up paying more (with shipping and handling fees) than it is worth new. (3) Toy swap. Clean out and clean up your kid's toys that they have outgrown. Get together with some other parents and swap toys or buy/sell them at used prices. (4) Book Swap. Do you feel like you don't have enough space for all your children's books? Organize a book swap with a group of families or at your church. By including many families there will be a wide range of books including books for different ages, reading levels, and interests. And best of all, it doesn't cost a thing!

CHAPTER 10
Yard Sales

YARD SALES - Andrea

Yard sales are field trips for myself and my children. We think of it as a treasure hunt. You will be amazed at the treasures you find. The downside of this fact is that you need to focus on needs and not wants. We have had luck with clothes, tools, decorative items and appliances. Always check electrical items to be sure they work, and know the average price of any items that you would like to purchase. This knowledge helps you from overpaying and is helpful when haggling over the price. Walk away if you can't get the prices within 10–20% of the retail value.

YARD SALES - Elaine

The U.S. is the leader in countries where we have so much "stuff" that we need to spend extra money to rent a space to store it all. My reasoning suggests that most people spend more money on the rental space than what the items inhabiting it are worth. Think about it. If you rent a storage space for $80/month, after just one year you have invested almost $1,000 in storage alone . . . but does the monetary value of the items amount to anything close to the $1,000 you handed over? If you find yourself in this situation, find someone who needs those items now and give them to them, donate them to a charity and use it as a taxable donation, or have a yard sale. By the time you would have actually used the items again it would have been cheaper for you to buy them, and in the process you have helped someone else! It's a win win situation!

Now as for finding things at yard sales, the possibilities are endless. Clothes, toys, tools, home décor, holiday items, books, crafts, housewares, and yard equipment are just a few of the things you can find.

Most people know the area they live in at least a little. Plan out your yard sales that way. If you know that there is a neighborhood yard sale going on in a really nice area, you are more likely to find nicer things. But at the same time realize that most of the time the "higher class" areas are likely to have slightly higher prices. They are usually well within reason, but you will find some that are priced too high.

Personal Experience: We went to a yard sale where a lady was trying to sell her teenage daughter's clothes. We made it the first stop on our list that day since girls' 12's and 14's are hard to find. She had name brand jeans priced for $10 - $12 each. That is an outrageous price to pay at a yard sale! Brand new Wal-Mart jeans are the same price.

Here is a general rule of thumb for most yard sale items: Most of the prices should be at or dance around 10 % - 25% of the retail price. Obviously there will be things that sell for more and things that sell for less. Clothes and shoes generally go 10% and less, but yard tools, appliances, etc. can go for more (around 30%).

Personal Experience: Chris and I went to an estate sale and bought a full-sized upright freezer. It was approximately six years old and in perfect condition. The sellers even had the paperwork from when they purchased it. The paperwork showed the purchase price as $640. We bought it for $175. The retail price of the smallest brand new upright freezer in the store was over $300.

On another trip, a yard sale advertised a generator. We needed one because we didn't live inside the city limits and when the power went out we lost everything including water since we are on a well. We bought this generator, that could run the entire house, for $800. Retail, that kind of generator sold for well over $2,000!

As you start to yard sale, you will pick up on the basic value and acceptable pricing for items. One more yard sale tip. If you are going to have your own yard sale, free all your clothes from their prisonous boxes and take them off the ground. If you hang items up and display them on tables, people are more likely to look through them because they look more appealing. The more organized and the cleaner things are the more successfully they will sell.

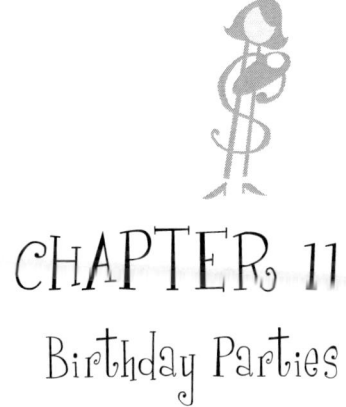

CHAPTER 11
Birthday Parties

BIRTHDAY PARTIES- Andrea

These are the times that make memories for our families. True? Absolutely! Every birthday at our house has been recorded on film and video, as were all of mine when I was a child. They truly are some of the happiest times for our family.

Happiest, however, does not necessarily equate with expensive. With the exception of one, we have done all of our birthday parties at home. We have found that this is the cheapest way. I have done birthday parties at home with a homemade cake, my own tablecloths, one balloon for the birthday child and decorating the tables with toys we already own.

For example, I used a Spiderman action figure for the centerpiece for a Spiderman party. We hand deliver any invitations that we possibly can to cut back even more. I also try to limit the number of guests to the age of the child. For example, a four year old can have four guests, a five year old, five. This number excludes siblings and cousins. One-year-old birthday parties are limited to family only to prevent the birthday child from becoming overwhelmed.

I'm sure you are wondering how I handle goody bags. I don't even remember such things as goody bags when I was young. I have found that my children don't even consider a party a party unless there are goody bags handed out. I always discuss with my children on the way to a party that they are not to ask for a goody bag, nor expect them. However, I must confess I have fallen prey to this tradition. (Okay, I know you are calling me spineless right now. I'm writing louder so that I cannot hear you.) Before you lose complete respect for me, I have managed to bag the bag in goody bags. I usually go to a dollar store and buy one item for each guest.

I also schedule birthday parties so that I do not feel compelled to serve a meal, for example 2:00 to 4:00 or 6:30 to 8:00. This way I only need to serve cake, ice cream and a drink. Activities are limited to games that we can utilize ordinary household items. For example:

> Bug party: caught fireflies
>
> Construction party: played with dump truck in a sandbox

Crocodile Hunter party: tackled an alligator float on a slip and slide

Ball party: played with a yard full of balls

Reptile party: had a friend bring reptiles to the house and had a "touch and share" time

Sleepover party: one person closes his/her eyes while all the others jump in any sleeping bag. The person then feels the sleeping bag and tries to determine the identity of the person in the bag

Bug party: did a treasure hunt of plastic bugs that we already owned

Scooby Doo party: used a picture of the gang and asked trivia questions about the series

Games are something you and your child can have a ball planning together. Be creative!

My parties cost at most $40. That certainly beats the $100 to $125 minimum that I have seen at most farmed-out birthday parties. You can do it. Before you say you do not have the time, remember you won't be employed anymore. You will have the time. Of course, when you are planning, don't overlook obvious resources like family members that have a pool or farm that you could utilize for free.

A note about gift-giving for birthday parties. When my son was three years old, he was invited to eight birthday parties within a six-week period. It dawned on me that our monthly budget was greatly impacted by gifts. We needed to decide as a family just how much we could afford to spend. Early on, I was spending $15 to $25 on non-family birthday presents. We decided that we could no longer afford to keep this up. We now purchase non family gifts for under $10. It is family policy. I always have my eyes open for good sale items that I can purchase in advance and store. This takes some organization, but it certainly simplifies gift-giving and keeps cost down.

BIRTHDAY PARTIES - Elaine

I grew up only having family parties, so I'm not particularly inclined to feel the need to throw my children a "friends" party every year. Chris and I came up with several nice alternatives rather than an annual birthday party. Our first alternative was to rotate birthday parties from year to year. We have three children, so if Leah has a birthday party in 2000, then Amber would have one in 2001 and Tess would have one in 2002, etc. Our second alternative was to offer our child something smaller but more special. We would let them invite one or two friends out to dinner or have a friend sleep over.

Before I go in depth on the subject of birthday parties here are a couple of basic suggestions:

- Don't have a party for a child that is three or younger. At that age, children can't appreciate what is going on. It is really more for the parents than the child.

• Don't go overboard and spend $100 or more on the party. If you do, you will have to outdo it next year because your child will expect it.

• Limit the number of children invited. Party supplies come in packs of eight . . . seems like a reasonable limit to me.

Okay, you are trying to plan your child's birthday party. Do you think you have to spend $50 or $100? Not a chance. The parties that I've given for the kids have been less than $30. That includes cake, party favors, games, decorations, and invitations. Here are some tips on keeping the cost down.

• Invitations. Invitations can be expensive if you order them or buy them in the store and mail them out to your guests. A great way trim the Invitation budget is to make them on your computer (either card or postcard style), let your child make their own invitations, or simply to invite the guests by phone or in person. If you decide to make an invitation, consider hand delivering it instead of mailing it.

• Birthday Cake. The birthday cake is my favorite part! I love to make and decorate my family's birthday cakes. I would much rather spend the time making my child's cake than call a store and spend $15 - $20 for a sheet cake. Making the cake is a labor of love for me. I want them to know that they are so special that I am willing to take two hours out of a busy schedule to do something just for them. I can usually make a decorated cake for less than $5. Here are several examples. Note: the first amount is the approximate regular cost for all of the items, while the second amount is the cost if you shop the sales.

Barbie–Cost $4.00 ($2.50) Cake mix, frosting, and a Barbie doll (we already owned)

Ladybug–Cost $6.50 ($4.50) Cake mix, red food coloring, frosting, and thin mints

Octopus–Cost $ 8.00 ($5.00) Cake mix, frosting, and gummy lifesavers

Kitty–Cost $6.00 ($4.00) Cake mix, frosting, shaved (colored) coconut and some M&Ms

Rainbow–Cost $5.00 ($3.50) Cake Mix, frosting and food coloring

Horse–Cost $4.00 ($2.50) Cake mix, frosting, and licorice

I have even made a 3-D sea turtle that fed over 50 people for less than $20! You can make some very special cakes if you are just willing to try. Remember, it doesn't need to look professional. Your kids will just be thrilled you made it!

Games. Kids love to play games at parties and usually you don't have to spend a lot of money on them. As you think of games, try to use things you already have. There are so many game ideas. The following examples are given just to get you thinking. If you would like to get more inexpensive ideas I recommend checking out parenting magazines and books from your local library. Just remember to do simple games, like games you played when you were a kid.

Idea #1 My sister-in-law, Amy, planned a reptile birthday party for her seven-year-old. For the games she bought a bucket of plastic lizards and frogs at the dollar store. Amy and her daughter made "profile" cards for them that included interesting facts and a picture. Then she and her daughter hid them around the back yard. Each child was given one or two profile cards and was instructed to find only the reptile on the card. If they found someone else's they had to leave it alone and keep looking. Once the kids found their items, they put them in bug boxes (purchased from the dollar store) with their names painted on them.

Idea #2 For the second game/activity Amy had a slip-n-slide and a crocodile float (like the ones for the pool). Each boy got to take turns wrestling the crocodile down the slip-n-slide. They had a blast! Both activities and their take home gift (the bug boxes) cost approximately $10.

Idea #3 For my daughter's 5th birthday party, I took yarn (a different color for each guest) and strung it all around the back yard. By the time I finished with all the yarn the back yard looked like a very colorful spider web. Each child was assigned a color and was told to follow the string, unraveling as they went. At the end of each string was their party favor (a purple baseball cap with painted flowers and bees).

Idea #4 My daughter went to a birthday party where the mother gathered old prom and bridesmaid's dresses (some purchased from a thrift shop), funny shoes and some costume jewelry. Then each girl got to pick out a dress. After dressing, each one received a makeover and hairstyling. Dad then came in and took pictures on the digital camera and printed them out. Upon leaving each girl received a framed picture of her "glamour shot." The picture frames were bought from the dollar store.

Idea #5 A friend from church, Lisa, had some face painting and carnival-like games at her daughter's party. She made up a board that showed their choices for face painting. (Choose simple things like balloons, rainbows, pompoms, hearts, etc.) Each child was then able to pick the item they wanted— this is definitely a crowd pleaser!! Some inexpensive carnival games include beanbag toss, milk bottle toss, clothespin in a jar, pin the nose on the clown, etc.

Party Favors. I understand the frustration parents have when it comes to children expecting a bag when they leave a birthday party. Like Andrea, I can only remind my children that this day is about the child we are going to visit and they should not expect anything. On the other hand, when we invite children over for a party, I like to give them something. This is why: it helps my child not to be greedy. You see, before the party we have looked for something we think the guests will enjoy. At the party, my child has received numerous gifts. Instead of the day being all about my child (gimmee, gimmee, gimmee), they *give* their guests a gift before they leave. We don't make a big deal about it, but it's another subtle teaching moment.

Here are several great ideas for party favors.

Decorated baseball cap, bag, or box

For a sleep over–decorate and personalize pillowcases

Journal books (with a pen or pencil)

Bug boxes–decorated and personalized

Framed picture of the child or picture of the child and birthday child together.

Book

Bracelets (could be something they made at the party as an activity)

Decorations (plates, cups, napkins, tablecloths, etc.). Sometimes more can be spent on decorations than on any other part of the party. Why? Most of the time the children don't care if everything matches. But if you are like me, you like to have it look right. Don't spend extra money on themed decorations (unless you get them on a great sale, of course). Buy a plain color that coordinates with the theme.

Let's say your child wanted a Bob the Builder

party. Instead of buying all themed decorations, consider buying blue and yellow plates, cups, napkins, etc. Then use some of your child's dump trucks and toy machines as decorations on the table. Try to make a cake that looks like Bob or maybe make a hardhat for the birthday cake. If you want wall decorations, buy a poster, print off pictures from the Internet or take a coloring book and crayons and color away! Remember they are children; you are not out to impress the parents. Some matchbox cars (dump trucks, earth movers, etc.) or plastic hard hats make great party favors. The hard hats can even be used as part of the table decorations.

Maybe your daughter would like to have a princess party. You can decorate the table with a tablecloth, organza, glitter, and ribbons. Princess hats that you and your child made and decorated (party favor the girls could take home) could be placed at each seat. You could even make a princess cake to top it all off.

Gifts for Birthday Parties. First of all, our kids don't go to every birthday party they are invited to. We generally limit it to kids from church and a couple of good friends at school. That helps us cut down on buying a bunch of gifts in the first place.

Next, we limit the money spent on gifts to approximately $8. I know you are thinking that is not very much, but when you shop the sales $8 goes a long way. I am always on the lookout for clearance items. I keep a box in my closet that is usually stocked pretty well so that when the girls are invited to a party, they can pick from a number of things.

Note: If you go into a specialty shop and see something you really like, consider buying several of them and asking for an additional discount.

Personal Experience: Chris and I were out on a date and walked into a specialty kids store. There they had a clearance area that was 50% off. I spotted a kit that would allow the kids to paint a terracotta pot with suggested designs. It included all the paint, brushes, sponges, the pot itself and the designs. Normally they were sold for $20 each, but were on sale for $10. I loved the idea for the kids and decided to ask the manager if she would sell them to me for $8 each if I bought them all. She said yes and we walked out of there with all 7 of them.

CHAPTER 19
Holidays

HOLIDAYS - Andrea

Oh, these times can be so tempting. Christmas especially is an expensive time for most families. The Christmas items are hitting the shelves before Halloween in most stores. Not only that, but shopping for Christmas has become an all-year endeavor for many families. This is a great time to get back to the true meaning of Christmas. We have instituted the three gift policy. If it was good enough for the King of Kings, then it is good enough for our children. We instruct our children that they will receive three gifts. Extremely expensive gifts are family gifts and must be shared (for example, trampolines, game cubes, battery-operated jeeps). We also encourage drawing names and putting monetary limits on gift-giving. This is very useful at keeping costs down within family gift-giving. Michael and I many times do not give each other gifts. It is refreshing to wake on Christmas morning and count our many blessings. Of course, Christmas would not be Christmas if we didn't do for others less fortunate. This is a time when your money can really give you a sense of personal satisfaction. And remember, keep it in line with the rest of your spending. Do not overdo it.

Referring back to the financial section: You should have a Christmas budget. Be sure to take your budget and Christmas list and decide how the money will be allotted. If you do not have a Christmas budget, decide what you have to spend (without using credit) and be creative. Do not hesitate to tell family and friends that you will be unable to exchange gifts this year if you are unable to pay cash for gifts. Or suggest an alternative such as a homemade gift that costs no more than $10. Remember, Christmas is about our Savior's birth. Debt distracts us from the true meaning; don't let it ruin your Christmas!

I utilize *Family Fun* constantly during the holiday seasons. From homemade Halloween costumes to interesting Easter decorations and really cool valentines, I can always find something unique, inexpensive and child friendly.

Halloween Costumes:

Incredible Hulk– Purple pants from a consignment shop, hand-me-down green sweatshirt with muscles drawn on it, and face paint.

Batman–Handmade cape and headpiece (made by a friend) and black sweat suit underneath.

Robin–Red sweatshirt, green sweatpants, and homemade green cape with a foam "R" glued to the shirt.

Peter Pan–Green felt shirt and pants loosely sewn together without hems and a belt and knife set from the dollar store.

The Cat in the Hat–A big black jumpsuit, a hat we already had in the toy box, face paint, and white gloves.

Easter ideas:

Use baskets you already own

Use same plastic eggs every year

We got rid of the grass (the boys always made a mess with it)

Easter baskets are kept simple with a few candy items. No expensive toys such as videos or computer games. We don't want to make Easter a mini-Christmas.

As always, buy any decorations after the holiday and store for the next year. Each year you will have something new to enjoy.

HOLIDAYS - Elaine

When it comes to Christmas and Easter, Chris and I as Christian parents want our children to know that these holidays are celebrated to remind us of Christ and his sacrifice for us. This is what is most important to us during these holidays. Now of course, no one can remove themselves from all the commercialism that goes on during these times. And to be honest, I enjoy shopping for people and giving them gifts. But, from the standpoint of this book, how can we spend less during the holidays and use this time as an opportunity to teach our children some wonderful life lessons? We need to find ways to trim the budget (being savvy shoppers always on the lookout for a good deal) and use the golden opportunities that holidays can bring to mold our children into individuals whose focus is not always on themselves.

You have stopped working outside the home because you want to be at home full-time with your kids, spend more time with them, and instill in them good morals and values. Take a couple of suggestions from below and savor the full value of your decision.

First of all, SLOW DOWN. The way to show your family and friends how important they are is to spend time with them. In this day and age someone stopping what they are doing to just spend time with you is worth far more than any gift they can buy. Remember this with your children, family and friends. Instead of running around nonstop from one program to another between Thanksgiving and New Years, pick out a handful of things that are important (yes, that means skipping some church and school events) and leave extra time for those special people you love. Enjoy a slower holiday pace with your children this year.

Also, don't forget to plan things that you and your children can do together that get them thinking about others. Plan a morning serving others, have the children clean out some of their things (that are still in good condition) and donate them, purchase food items and take them to a local food pantry. Give your children an opportunity to see how blessed they are and how they can give something back.

Gifts

In our family, each child will typically receive three Christmas gifts. We really don't feel the need to do more than that because besides us, our children can receive gifts from more than eight other extended family members. We also limit the amount of money spent on each family member. Now, I know parents who spend hundreds of dollars each year on Christmas gifts for their children. I can understand when children get older that the things you may want to get them for Christmas are slightly more expensive, but when your children are young, they don't need to get $200 or $300 worth of gifts. Our children are all fairly young and I can't recall having ever spent more than $50 on each child for Christmas gifts.

One more reason to limit the number of gifts—take a look at your house (or your friends' house). I bet there are not only toys crammed in every nook and cranny, but boxes in the attic and garage too. How many do the kids actually play with? Very few I'm sure. Most of the time toys are played with for a couple of weeks and then forgotten or discarded for something new. Here are a couple of non-toy ideas: Have they been asking to redecorate their room? Tell them to write specific things down for their list. Are they bugging you about going to summer camp? That is an excellent thing to put their birthday or Christmas money toward. Have your kids been begging you for a tree fort? Buy some wood, put a bow on it and spend some time working on it together. So start thinking outside that brightly-colored overpriced toy box.

Most of our parents/grandparents don't need more knickknacks around the house. Many of them might be on limited incomes. If that is the case, consider items that are less costly or things that could be very useful for them like calendars with family pictures, subscriptions to magazines they enjoy, an extended subscription to the newspaper, gift certificates to places they frequent, photo refrigerator magnets the kids made, or themed gift baskets (movie, golf, bath . . . use your imagination!). If they really have everything and don't need more things, make a donation to a charity in their name and then give them a card that explains what you have done.

Also, in our families we exchange names at Christmas instead of buying for everyone. Adults exchange with adults and children exchange with children. We also set limits on gifts. Talk with your family and agree on an amount. I strongly encourage you to do this. It is a huge money saver and you will probably be able to see what people are opening instead of the normal sea of wrapping paper flying everywhere.

Teachers. Your child's teacher is someone to be appreciated. Most of us like to buy them something at Christmas and at the end of the year. But if you are unable to afford a gift, send them a note thanking them for all their hard work and dedication. I'm sure that a heartfelt thank you never goes unappreciated. If you can give them something, instead of giving your child's teacher another mug or desk ornament, give them something they need for their classroom. Try asking them how much of their own money they spend on their classroom. I'll bet that they spend several hundred dollars. If you aren't sure what they need, ask. Most of them have a wish list. So, give them something for their classroom or give them a gift certificate that they can use for themselves.

Thank you notes. Here's a great idea that my friend Amy uses at Christmas when her children are sending their thank you notes out for gifts they have received. Save the Christmas cards you receive from year to year. Tear off the front of the card with the picture and let your children write their thank yous on the back of it. People rarely write on that part of the card. All you need then is an envelope and a stamp. What a great way to recycle, save money, and encourage your children to be thankful!

Decorations and Holiday Savings

In the following paragraphs I will tell you about some cheap decorating ideas and ways you can save money during holidays. Please remember that you are decorating for your kids, not to impress adults. Your kids will have more fun and enjoy decorations they help create. There are many wonderful seasonal ideas that I have found in *Family Fun* magazine. It is a wonderful resource for inexpensive ideas of things to do with your children. I recommend checking it out.

Winter. Spend some time making paper snowflakes and snowmen. They can be kept up all through the winter even after Christmas. Another thing that my children had lots of fun doing was painting the windows. Let them paint winter or holiday scenes on your windows with regular children's paint. It comes off with window cleaner and a rag. Also, the week after Christmas (or any other holiday for that matter) is an ideal time to add to your Christmas decorations without hurting your wallet. Just remember to leave a little extra money set aside expressly for that purpose.

Valentine's Day. Pull out the construction

paper and cut out hearts. Let the kids add their own valentine messages to them. Hang them on the walls, refrigerator, doors, and windows. Don't bother buying pre-made cards for your children to give to their classmates and friends; sit down with them and make homemade Valentine's cards. It's a great money saver and an especially good way to spend some time with your kids.

As for Mom's and Dad's Valentine's gifts, replace those high-priced candy and flowers with a date. Hire a babysitter and go to a movie, have dinner, or go to a local coffee house that plays live music. Time spent with your spouse is much more valuable than that box of candy.

Easter. Cut out construction paper in the shape of eggs and let your kids paint or color them. You can even let them cut out other shapes and glue them on the egg or add stickers and glitter to them. Easter eggs and that wonderful green plastic grass that goes inside Easter baskets can be reused year after year, so don't throw it away. Also, try not to get new baskets each year. Instead get one nice one, maybe even with your child's name on it, and reuse it each year. Lastly, you don't need to buy egg dying kits. All you need is vinegar, water and some food coloring.

Halloween. Instead of just decorating for Halloween, consider putting up things that are more "fallish" and adding a couple of Halloween touches so that after Halloween you can use most of the decorations all the way through Thanksgiving. For example, a painted pumpkin lasts much longer than a carved one does, and if they only paint one side then you can turn it around and use it for weeks after Halloween. You can bring out that paint again and let them have fun on the windows. Construction paper and crayons are always great for leaves, pumpkins, spiders, etc. Quilt batting stretched out makes wonderful spider webs—and you don't need very much at all. Lastly, don't forget that you can always let the kids use nature itself to decorate with (dried leaves, pine cones, etc.).

While we are on the subject of Halloween, let's talk about costumes. Don't buy pre-made costumes at the store. They are worn for two or three hours on one night and most likely never used again. Try to use your child's clothing as a base and build a costume from it or keep your eyes out at yard/garage sales for the pre-made costumes. We have found several pre-made costumes that way and only paid a couple dollars for them. With a little imagination and a couple of inexpensive craft/sewing supplies, you can transform and child wearing all one color clothing into a myriad of superheroes, animals, and bugs, to name a few. We transformed our youngest daughter into a princess by putting her in one of her sister's white dresses that had no waistline, adding a ribbon around her chest and giving her a princess hat that we had in the dress up box. Another daughter wore all black, put white socks on her hands, pinned on a stuffed sock for a tail, added felt ears to a hair band, and painted her face up to make herself a cat. Encourage your child to be part of the process of creating their costume. You can also check out issues of *Family Fun* and other parenting magazines for Halloween costume ideas. They regularly give ideas in their fall/Halloween issues.

Chapter 13
Family Fun for Less

FAMILY FUN FOR LESS-Andrea

The key to family fun is being together. Your children will always remember your interactions, but not necessarily the most expensive events. You would be amazed at the simple and inexpensive activities you can do to have family fun. Ideas are as follows:

After the yard clippings have piled up during fall and spring yard work, we build a bonfire and roast hot dogs and s'mores.

Family game night. Just an ordinary board or card game with popcorn and drinks. A whole lot of bragging and embellishing adds to the fun!

Outdoor concerts and fireworks are free in areas during the summertime.

One family shared with me that they sleep in

sleeping bags in the family room on Friday nights. Their children always look forward to this time.

We go for family bike rides together now that everyone can ride a bike. It has actually become a neighborhood event since all the neighbors' children want to join in on the fun.

Bible study time. I read a Bible story each night at supper. Michael and I enjoy and value teaching Biblical principles and the children enjoy trying to guess what is going to happen next.

FAMILY FUN FOR LESS- Elaine

The mentality on fun for many families is, "The more it costs, the more fun we will have." In most cases this couldn't be further from the truth. Below is an example of the different levels of expense for a family of four to enjoy dinner or dessert and a movie.

> Most expensive: Dinner out (4 @ 8.50 = $34); 7 pm theater movie (4 @ $7 = 28) Total $62
>
> One step down: Matinee tickets (4 @ 4.50 = $18); Ice cream (at shop) 4 @ 2.50 = $10) Total $28
>
> Next step down: Rented movie ($4); pizza or subs ordered in ($15) Total $19
>
> Least expensive: Library movie ($0); homemade pizza, soda, rice krispies (under $12) Total $12

$ MILLION DOLLAR MOM $

Other ideas for cheap (or free) family fun:

Playground and a picnic
Bike trails
Feeding ducks at a local lake
Nature hikes
Fishing

Buy some plants/flowers/seeds. Let your children plant a garden and watch it grow.

The library (story time for young children, borrow books, DVD's, videos, CDs, and books on tape)

Family zoo pass (if you have a zoo fairly close by). Children never tire of the zoo so by the third time you visit in one year, you have most likely saved money. In North Carolina, a zoo pass also admits you into all the state aquariums.

Discount nights at your local Science and Discovery museums. Call to find out if your museum participates in discount nights.

Water Park. If you go to some water parks after 4 or 5 pm your pass will be good that day, plus the entire next day. Two days of fun for the price of one—stretch out that fun.

Personal Experience: While we were building our house we clamped down on extra spending. We had to say "no" to the girls' requests more than we liked. Chris was not at home much; working on the house and going back to his job most nights. We could begin to see the girls getting fussy, moody and a little depressed. I don't blame them; I felt the same way sometimes.

One day in November Chris and I agreed that the kids needed a "fun day." I picked the girls up from school and surprised them by telling them that we were just going to do fun things for the next two days. There was only one catch — we couldn't spend more than $30. I know what you're thinking, "I bet they didn't have *much* fun." Actually we had a blast, and it was a great learning experience for them too. The girls had to agree (or compromise) with each other, they had to tell me what they wanted to do, how much it cost, and how much we had left. This is what they decided to do:

1. Rent movies using a rent one get one free coupon. They watched one movie that night and the second movie the next day. Cost $4

2. Eat the dinner I had planned for that night instead of eating out. Cost $0

3. Buy a dessert at the grocery store (they bought a 24 value pack of popsicles and enjoyed them for many days to come). Cost $3.25

4. Swimming at the local aquatic center (we told some of their friends' parents that we were going. Their parents liked the idea and came too). Cost $7

5. Lunch at Ci-Ci's Pizza after swimming (their friends came too). Cost $13

Total cost for two days of fun for the four of us–$27.25!

Not only did they have a great time, but also they learned (without realizing it) how to budget, decide the best value for their money, compromise, and how to be grateful. We heard loads of "Thank yous." Their outlook after that was much better. It was a good lesson for us too. We needed to remember that everyone needs a reprieve every once in a while from the financial stresses that we all face. Kids feel that stress too. We just need to make sure that we don't go overboard. It doesn't take a lot—just a little creativity and change in thinking.

CHAPTER 14
Vacations

VACATIONS-Andrea

Ah, the All-American dream—a nice vacation. When you are a stay-at-home mom, vacations can seem like an indulgence. Not in my book. Vacations are a necessity. They refresh, renew, and reconnect the family. Whatever you do, do not forgo the vacation. When you are a stay-at-home mom, vacations need to be cost-effective and creative. So where does the money come from? First you need to decide how much you need and how much you can afford to spend. Michael and I have a vacation/Christmas fund that we contribute to monthly. We know exactly how much we have to spend. If we need more, we know we have to cut back somewhere else or have a yard sale.

Now that you know what you have to spend, where do you want to go? The beach? The mountains? If your children are not in school, off-season trips are inexpensive. Do you have family near some of these places that you can visit? Would you consider camping? (Children are not quite as attached to modern amenities as adults are.)

When looking for accommodations, be sure to choose somewhere that has at least one of the following:

- Children eat free

- Free continental breakfast

- Kitchenette. By eating some meals in, the food budget can be greatly reduced.

Be wary of expensive tourist traps and enjoy the natural beauty of the places you are visiting. Be sure to prepare children that they will see advertising for these places but you have chosen other special places equally as exciting. Or, allow children to plan activities within a specified budget. Remember, vacations are to be relaxing, so playing by the ocean or in a forest needs no other activities.

Souvenirs are another issue needing attention. We started "The Courtesy Cup," an idea I got from *Family Fun*. Each child decorates his/her own cup. When the child is caught being kind, respectful or compassionate towards another family member, a quarter is placed in his/her cup. At vacation time, the amounts are tallied and the children use this money to purchase a souvenir of choice. This method eliminates the "I wanna's" and keeps the souvenir purchasing to a minimum.

Good luck planning your next vacation, and remember, vacations are a necessity.

VACATIONS - Elaine

Many people feel a week long vacation away or a trip to a major theme park is necessary. I prefer several short vacations as opposed to one long one. After three or four days I am ready to sleep in my own bed. Whatever you decide to do for a vacation just make sure you make a budget and stick to it. We have found several ways to stretch our vacation dollar. Read the following paragraphs and see if you can implement any of these on your next vacation.

Discount Tickets. There are almost always discount tickets to be found for one reason or another for theme parks. Take a little time and find out when there are specials going on and then try to plan your visit within that time frame if at all possible.

Meals on the road. Pack a cooler with your lunch, snacks and drinks and stop and have a picnic instead of stopping at the fast food restaurant. It's cheaper and healthier. When you are getting ready to come back home, stop at the grocery store and pick up a couple things for the cooler.

Lodging. Try to go off-season if that will work with your schedules. If you are going to a big vacation or theme park area, try staying a little further out. Driving the extra 30 minutes could save you on the price of the hotel. If you are going to stay in a hotel, spend a little extra to get a room with an efficiency kitchen, or at least a microwave and refrigerator. You can save a lot of money over several days by having cereal, donuts, or yogurt for breakfast and keeping lunch meats in the fridge for lunch. That microwave will come in handy when you want some popcorn at night.

Travel Breaks. If you are driving more than five or six hours to your destination, break the trip up by scouting out a neat stop over. Maybe a factory that has tours or a museum or historic sight. It becomes part of the vacation, it's relatively inexpensive, and it breaks up the driving.

Souvenirs. We don't typically buy souvenirs for our kids. Most of the time we take pictures and put them in each child's photo album to help them remember the time. If you can get some on sale, consider giving your older children a disposable camera so they can take some pictures themselves. Just make sure you take pictures also, since their pictures might not show what they expected. A couple of times our children have been allowed to buy a souvenir that they either pay all or part of. This is a good way to teach them the value of money.

Personal Experience: One of the fund raisers our children's school participated in rewarded them with a free ticket to Six Flags. They both earned their tickets and then my husband and I were able to get BOGO tickets. We packed lunch in a cooler to eat in the car and only bought a drink that could be refilled inside the park. We went with my brother and his family (splitting the cost of a special device to reserve our place in the long lines). Instead of it costing us $230+ for the day, we were able to get in, eat lunch, have drinks in the park, and splurge on the Qbot for a total of $100!

Just a couple of mini-vacation ideas to get you thinking:

1. Drive to the mountains overnight and hike or (in Nov/Dec) cut down your Christmas tree the next morning.

2. Make an overnight trip to the beach or rent a beach house with another family member or friend. You can then split the cost.

3. Go camping, hiking or fishing.

4. Visit a state park or historic site.

5. Visit family or friends that are out of town and just hang out together (maybe plan one or two special activities). The kids will probably have more fun just playing with other kids—no matter what the activity.

CHAPTER 15
Entertaining

ENTERTAINING – Andrea

I am a people person and I love having people around me. My home is a place where my children's friends come regularly. As much as I love this, I have to recognize that school-age kids can eat you out of house and home. I keep frozen pops in the freezer (you know the ones you can buy 100 for approximately $3). I also only serve water. I keep all of those lovely free plastic cups from every restaurant in town and store them in a child-convenient location. I also keep a bag of carrots. If a visitor is really hungry, he may have a carrot. This keeps my house from being the supper spoiling place.

I was recently involved in hostessing a 50th wedding anniversary and a bridal shower. Both events were on a budget. We booked the events at the churches where the guests of honor were members. I was able to utilize tables, chairs, tablecloths, punch bowls, etc. These items cut down on rental costs as well as a facility rental. Each time we made the food (remember, I come from a long line of great cooks). I must confess that I hosted the bridal shower with a good friend that is a pastry chef. Now that's what I call utilizing resources! In addition, we had connections with a florist who gave us a deal. All of these ideas saved us greatly in the end and we were able to provide two elegant and classy events. The key is knowing what you have to spend and sticking to it.

ENTERTAINING - Elaine

You may feel as though you cannot entertain since your income has been reduced. While you might not be able to entertain as often or have catered events, you are certainly still able to throw a nice party. Just remember, you are home now so make decorations, plan out early what you want to eat, buy things on sale, and make most of the food yourself.

Example #1 A couple of years ago my brother and sister-in-law, John and Amy, were throwing a party. Amy sent out invitations she made on the computer to more than 100 people. They wanted their guests to leave the party well fed and with many fond memories. John smoked brisket (sale price $.99/lb), and grilled chicken breasts (BOGO) and hot dogs (Sam's Club). Amy shopped the sales and made appetizers including chips and homemade salsa, pasta salad, baked beans, potato chips, peach and blackberry cobbler, and drinks. Total cost for this party? Approximately $200. That's less than $2 per person!

Example #2 I hosted a baby shower for my sister. For decorations we used a tablecloth I already had, hand picked flowers and put them in small baby bottles (from my stash), placed wooden alphabet baby blocks on the table (our toys), and used pastel colored streamers and a crib (one of the gifts). My china plates and silverware were used along with my sister-in-law's goblets and glass dessert cups for the place settings. Since we all wanted to buy nice gifts for Christine and her husband, the food was split between several of us. After lunch and gifts we enjoyed a couple hours of scrapbooking. I use this as an example to show you that a party can be very enjoyable yet cost very little because no one person must pay for it all. Many things that are already owned can be utilized.

Invitations. Instead of purchasing or having invitations printed, do it yourself. There are many computer programs today that have cards and invitations at your disposal. All you have to do is pick the type of card, enter your information, and put card stock in your printer. Don't forget that you can save money on stamps if you make the invitation in the form of a postcard. If you don't like the idea of a postcard, you can print out cards and hand deliver them. Or, if the invitation can be more informal, just call them up and invite them personally.

Decorations. If you have a theme for a party, try to decorate with creative ideas from that theme. For example, if you are having a party in the fall, have your kids gather leaves, press them and then use them for table decorations. Buy pumpkins, gourds, and Indian corn after Halloween and make a couple of centerpieces. For winter paint your pumpkins white, cluster them, and make them into snowmen. Also for winter, don't forget about pine cones, holly and wreaths. If you have some nice glass bowls, put some floating candles in water and then throw in some fresh cranberries. Add a few sprigs of extra Christmas tree limbs around the bowl and you have a beautiful table decoration.

Food. Now that you are staying at home, you can make some of the party food yourself instead of ordering it. Try to plan food that you can make at least partially before hand. Warehouse clubs offer many items that are partially or totally prepared. With some, all you have to do is heat them up and lay them out on a decorative dish. They offer a way to get catered-type food at a lower price. Obviously if it is a very informal party, you may receive offers from guests to bring something. Don't be shy about taking them up on their offer.

CHAPTER 16
Babysitting

BABYSITTING - Andrea

Now that your child is no longer in daycare, childcare can pose many issues. But once again, creativity is your ally. First, get to know other stay-at-home moms and determine the ones with similar values as you. These are good folks to trade off childcare needs. After that, teenagers are great resources for nights and weekends. Make sure you know them and their families well in order to be confident of their skills. I personally require a driver's license, CPR certification and good "think on your feet" kinds of skills. I want an individual that knows what to do in an emergency. As a mother and nurse, I realize those first few minutes of an emergency are critical to the outcome. I bet you are asking, "So what do you pay?" I don't have a clear cut answer for that one. I have seen all types of ways to pay a babysitter and anywhere from $2 per child per hour to $12/hour. I recommend at least minimum wage and upwards. You are probably saying, "That's not frugal at all!" IT ISN'T. This one is an issue of principle. If our children are so precious and valuable to us, then we need to pay our sitters accordingly. We certainly do not need to pay someone to mow our lawn more than we need to pay someone to keep our children. That devalues the mothers that choose to stay at home with them. So please hear me when I say—value your sitters as the folks who are caring for the most precious people in your life. I realize by paying more you may limit the frequency of your dates, but remember you always have other moms with whom you can trade. More importantly, you are raising the standard of care you are providing for your children. Remember, they are worthy of this. In addition, this increases your value as a stay-at-home mom—priceless!

    One more tidbit that you may find helpful: periodically someone wants to give you a present and they don't know what to get you or maybe they don't have much to spend. One suggestion you can offer is for them to babysit for free. When one of our babysitters was in college and wanted to give our family a gift, we suggested a night out. Our boys loved spending time with her and Michael and I certainly appreciated the night out. This is also a great gift to ask for from grandparents.

BABYSITTING - Elaine

    Chris and I don't hire babysitters often. We usually swap with other parents or use family members when they are willing. This keeps our costs down. We do, however, occasionally hire a babysitter. My major requirement is that the sitter is from our church. By hiring a teen or college student from our church I have had the opportunity to observe them (their actions, reactions and behaviors in general), get recommendations from other trusted Christians within the church that have had them babysit, and get to know the babysitter's parents and what their parents expect from them. With this information, I can feel confident that the potential babysitter has a good head on her shoulders, has my children's best interests in mind, and is a good role model for my girls to look up to.

    I know that while I don't know every situation that my children will be in, God does. His sovereignty and protection surrounds them and all I can do is make sure that I provide my children with the best care using my best judgment.

    As for payment, pay them as much as you can, especially if you and your kids like them and you want them to come back. If they are the kind of babysitter you want, you need to be the kind of "employer" that they want to come back to. Also make sure you take into consideration if they are preparing meals for the kids, have the kids awake all or the majority of the time, and if they provide their own transportation. Those things are usually worth more to us.

One more thing. We have tried to pay our babysitters well (although not always well enough), but if you are not able to pay them what you really want to, try to do something else special for them. At Christmas, birthday or a graduation buy them a small gift or give them a gift certificate; buy two tickets to a movie theater (make sure it's okay with their parents) and tell them to treat themselves and a friend to a movie; put together a good old-fashioned care package. In the end you don't have to spend a lot of money, just let them to know that they are appreciated.

CHAPTER 17
Furniture & Decorating

FURNITURE & DECORATING - Andrea

Oh how I love to decorate! This is another area that I can go overboard; however, it certainly isn't necessary. Just watch shows like Trading Spaces and you will see that decorating ideas do not always require large amounts of cash.

First of all, do you have too much furniture? A common decorating mistake is using too much furniture in a room. The best way to redecorate a room is to take all of the furniture out and add it back in one item at a time according to the purpose of the room. Once the room feels balanced, purposeful, and uncluttered—STOP. Do not continue to add items. Continue the process throughout the house. Then take all the extra items and discard them (whether by selling them or giving them away).

Do not rent a storage building to store items. If you truly believe that one day you will have a house large enough for these items, then consider loaning them to a family member or friend that may be in need of temporary furniture.

Once you have uncluttered the house, decide on the colors that you want to use in the room. Keep your color swatches in your purse and keep your eyes out for items at yard sales, family discards, discount sales, etc. When birthdays and Christmas roll around, decorations are great gift ideas.

Once you have completed a room, do not go back to it. Leave it as it is. Remember, it is okay to take your time decorating a room. The end result will be rewarding after you have invested so much of yourself.

If you are not good with colors, ask a friend with a knack for this. Trust me, she will be flattered that you asked. In addition, be willing to attempt to sew, paint, and build items. If you truly do not have any of these gifts, be willing to trade off services with gifted friends. For example, offer to clean someone's house several times for the making of some curtains. Also, if a friend has a gift you want to learn, organize a group of ladies and allow her to teach the group as a "girls' night out" activity. Networking like this will open all sorts of doors for you in terms of meeting your decorating goals. Good luck and remember—no clutter!

FURNITURE & DECORATING - Elaine

My main suggestion for decorating is to look at ideas you like in magazines, books, and on home decorating shows and figure out a way you can do them for cheaper by substituting. Also, visit the home tours that are popular in many cities. They are great places to get ideas. Take notes and then go home and figure out how you can achieve the same look for less.

As for furniture, simplify and make your furniture do double-duty. Instead of a changing table, buy dresser and a changing pad. Instead of a coffee table, buy a chest or steamer trunk and use it for storage. Don't have room for a guest bed? Buy a sleeper sofa. You get the idea.

Spend the money on closet organizers. You will be able to use every inch of your closets efficiently and have more hanging space. The more you hang, the less room you need in dressers. Maybe you can get one of those extra dressers out of your room. The less furniture the better.

Paint, paint, paint! You've heard it before, paint is the cheapest way to transform a room. You can make a room appear bigger, smaller, cozy, formal, fun, airy, or calming just by changing the color. Another thing I like about paint is that if you decide you don't like it it only costs you another gallon or two to fix it. By the way, if you check out Consumer Reports you will find that you don't even need to spend big bucks on some of the "name brand" paints. Some of the regular brands work just as well. Check out a copy for yourself and save money on your next gallon of paint. Lastly, when you are painting and you have children, use semi-gloss. It makes cleaning all those little handprints so much easier!

Use basic accessories to bring a room together. My oldest daughter loves Garfield. Instead of buying the entire matching comforter set and all the expensive accessories, I painted her wall a neutral color and then projected Garfield images on the walls. My sister and I traced and painted them. We finished it off by making a red comforter with coordinating window valance and bought her a Garfield pillowcase. She received some Garfield knickknacks and a calendar from people for Christmas. And now her room gives the illusion of being a Garfield room without the expense.

CHAPTER 18
Miscellaneous

BREASTFEEDING - Andrea

So what does breastfeeding have to do with becoming a stay-at-home mom? Aside from decreasing childhood illnesses, improving eyesight, decreasing the chances of allergies, decreasing Attention Deficit Disorder and increasing IQ scores, it is all-around cheaper. Can you tell I'm a nurse and big fan of breastfeeding? I can go into an endless list of why you should breastfeed your baby, but for this book's purposes, it will save you big bucks. The average cost of a can of formula is $19 - $21.50. How much would *you* save each month? A child that breast feeds the first year, yes I said one year, has less doctor visits per year. All of this money saved will assist you in staying at home and will be bonused by all the previously mentioned advantages of breastfeeding your child.

HAIRCUTS – Elaine

When it comes to haircuts my philosophy is, "Don't spend money on something you can do easily yourself." I have three girls. All of their haircuts are simple, so I have the professional cut their hair, and then I trim it for *at least* the next three months. After that time I have the professional "fix" anything I have done in the previous months. By cutting their hair at least three out of every four months, we spend less than $120/year on kids' cuts instead of well over $360.

If you have boys you can do something similar. If they like the crew cut/shaved look then purchase some electric clippers and start cutting it yourself. My husband cuts his hair with clippers so we haven't had to pay for his hair to be cut in years.

For my hair I have found a lady at an inexpensive salon that has been cutting hair for years. I would recommend you do the same. Instead of paying $25 - $40 per month to get your hair cut, find a person that has been doing it for a long time at an inexpensive salon and spend only $15 - $20. Also, consider going every six weeks instead of every four—that's four less cuts to pay for every year.

By using these tips, instead of spending over $850 per year we spend less than $300 per year on haircuts for our family of five.

MILLION DOLLAR MOM

GARDENING - Andrea

This section could fall under two categories: family fun or groceries. This project is as much fun as it is utilitarian. My boys have learned so much about nature and how things grow. They know what is a ripe fruit or vegetable and what is not. They love running to the garden to see what has changed and what is ready to be picked. I love the way it cuts back on the grocery bills. Many times we decide what vegetables are for supper by what choices are ready to be eaten. When the vegetables start coming by the barrels, it is a great way to thank some of the special folks in your life. If you are thinking you need a lot of land to have a garden, you are wrong. Our garden is a 10' x 10' space. There are plenty of resources regarding flower box gardens, just check the Internet. For those of you who know nothing about gardening, it is very easy to learn and provides a summer full of entertainment for your children.

MEDICATIONS - Elaine

Buy the generic prescription drug or store brand of your over the counter medications. You can save several dollars on each bottle of medicine if you purchase the store brand. If you are not sure which ones match up, just check the ingredients on the back or ask the pharmacist. Most of the time the generics are sitting right next to the name brand medication on the shelf.

Make sure to watch the drug store ads when they come out. Sometimes you will see them running sales for BOGO on the store brand medications or they will run a 50% off coupon on all store brand over-the-counter medications. This is a great time to stock up!

Also, compare the prices at different drug stores. I have found that the same prescription medication does *not* cost the same amount at every drug store chain. I stumbled along this one by accident. I had been getting a prescription filled by one drug store chain. When we moved, I switched drug store chains to one that was closer to our home. The first store was charging me over $22 for a prescription, the second one only charged $18 for the same prescription. That is a $4 savings each month on one prescription. I called and checked on four other medications and found as much as a $10 difference on one medication. I can only imagine that there can be significant savings if several prescriptions are filled each month or if prescriptions are not covered under your medical plan.

CHAPTER 19
When an Emergency Strikes

WHEN AN EMERGENCY STRIKES – Andrea

I'm sure you are asking, what happens when things go wrong? How can a family survive when a truly devastating emergency occurs? What happens when dad is laid off, a family member is critically ill, or when expenses exceed the income for a long period of time? At first glance, these problems seem impossible to solve for a one-income family. However, looks can be detrimentally deceiving. A one-income family has an untapped resource that can be accessed at any time. This resource can be the difference between survival and disaster. So many families today find themselves in a financial disaster with all employable family members currently working to support the family in good financial times. When the finances cannot pay the bills, there is no one else to send into the work force. The single-income family has a trump card—the stay-at-home mom. The stay-at-home-mom can re-enter the work force at any time to replace any lost wages. She may or may not be able to earn as much, but many times her income in conjunction with unemployment, disability, and/or savings may be the difference between financial survival and bankruptcy. Sample this food for thought from *The Two Income Trap*, then seriously ponder the value of a stay-at-home mom.

> *A mother who has gone into the workplace brings home a paycheck, but she forfeits the economic value of her backup role. So long as nothing goes wrong, the trade off is a simple choice between two viable alternatives. Some families prefer to have Mom at home and are willing to live with less money; others accommodate a working mother and enjoy a richer lifestyle. When trouble strikes, however, the family learns that the two choices may not have been as equivalent as they had seemed. Only one leaves the family with a safety net. (Warren & Tyagi, 2003, pg. 62–63)*

I can personally say we have lived through a family emergency. It wasn't the kind as was described earlier, it was subtle and it caught our entire family by surprise. Michael had been offered a wonderful employment opportunity that required a move. The company of course paid our moving expenses but did not buy our home. We immediately put our house on the market, but a year later the house still had not sold. Fortunately, not only do Michael and I save for a rainy day, but we have faith in a God that cares for our needs. It was faith that would get us through this predicament. We were faced with two options: make more money or lower our bills. However, we had a resource that two-income families do not have—an employable family member. It was at times such as these when we realized we had made the right decision.

WHEN AN EMERGENY STRIKES - Elaine

It would be nice if once we made our plans and budgets everything continued on the way we planned them. But as we all know, unexpected events and emergencies occur. If we have been able to do all the right things and save at least three times our income then we have a good buffer. But if you do not have that buffer, one or two unexpected bills can seemingly mean disaster for a one-income family. As Andrea pointed out earlier, the stay-at-home mom is an invaluable financial resource who can re-enter the workforce.

Chris and I have been blessed to not have a debilitating emergency occur. But we have had enough things happen that we have had to consider me going back to work several times. Each time this has happened we have asked God for wisdom and guidance and repeated our desires for me to stay at home with the girls. He has always been faithful to answer our prayers, although not necessarily always in the way we expected. It did sometimes mean work in various forms.

If you find yourself in need of some supplemental income which will counteract an unexpected bill, don't panic and start looking for full- or even part-time work outside your home right away. Pull from your own resources first. If you have a job that allows for contract work from home like Web designing or writing articles, consider that option. Look at the things you love to do and are gifted in. These sources of income could include anything from bookkeeping, typing or music lessons to sewing, cleaning, shopping or decorating. Each of these jobs can produce extra income without taking you away from your children, which is what you desire most.

CHAPTER 20

Priceless

So just what are you worth? According to an unnamed life insurance ad, you total the wages of a childcare worker, housekeeper, cook, personal assistant, and chauffeur. Multiply that number by ten.

According to their ad, this dollar value is the amount of life insurance you need to replace a stay-at-home parent. Although I was impressed with the progressiveness of this ad, I felt the job description was rather sketchy. I decided to compile my own list using the U.S. Department of Labor, Bureau of Labor Statistics (May 2004). I realize that I may be reaching with some of my listed items, but I also recognize that my list is in no way complete. So enjoy yourself as you read this section.

Andrea English & Elaine Shepherd

Job	**Hourly Wage**

Counselor
(my children and all their friends) $18.21

Director, Religious Activities $16.14

Registered Nurse
(take into account shift differential) $26.06

Cook, Short order . . . . $ 8.46

Cook, Head Chef
(I do both at my house, what about you?) $16.42

Maid . . . . $ 8.62

Landscaping/Grounds keeping $10.62

Tree trimmer/pruner $13.37

Amusement/Recreation Attendant . . . . $ 8.00

Barber $12.04

Hairdresser $10.95

Manicurist/Pedicurist (not including tips) . . . . . . $ 9.65

Shampooer . . . . $ 7.51

Skin Care Specialist (all those lovely rashes) $13.20

Baggage Porter/Bellhop $10.46

Concierge $11.93

Tour Guide and Escort . . . . $ 9.92

Childcare Worker . . . . $ 8.57

Personal/Home Care Aide . . . . $ 8.38

Residential Adviser $11.17

MILLION DOLLAR MOM

Door-to-Door Sales
(Don't you love school fund raisers?) $13.36

Switchboard Operator
(including Answering Service). $10.81

Bookkeeping/Accounting $14.34

Courier/Messenger $10.26

Taper $19.25
(Okay, I'm getting out of hand. Do you know how much tape I use?)

Baker $10.97

Butcher/Meat Cutter. $13.12

Laundry/Dry Cleaning Worker . . . . $ 8.74

Pressers, Garment. . . . . $ 8.62

Shoe Repairer. . . . . $ 9.68

Sewer, hand $10.20

Tailer/Dressmaker $11.76

Taxi Driver/Chauffeur $10.34

Packer and Packager. . . . . $ 8.97

Purchasing Manager. $37.51

Budget Analyst. $28.41

Are you feeling important? You should. As a matter of fact, you are *priceless!*

Conclusion

Well, you made it. What did you think? Does it all seem foreign to you? I'm sure at least some of it does, but you will be amazed at how easy it is once you get started. Elaine and I are in your corner rooting for you all the way. So if you are tired of being pulled limb from limb, overextended and frazzled, take the first step and have a heart-to-heart talk with your husband. There are many ways to make this happen. Just take it one step at a time. As Tammy Maltby and Tamra Furah put it in their book, *Lifegiving*:

> *Many women today are at war within themselves. The battlefield is our souls, and the casualties are often our marriages, children, and even our culture. If women are not caretakers, then who will be? If women stop nurturing, who will pick up the slack? If women do not begin compassionate social moments, who will?*
>
> *For nearly three generations, we have heard messages from movies, sitcoms, advertisements,*

and women's magazines about finding our value in work outside the home. Still, a majority of women today - if they believed they had a choice - would rather stay home with their pre-school-aged children than work. Yet very few do it without inner conflict over their perceived sense of self-worth.

Are you one of the pioneers who will pave the way back to immeasurable worth and respect, bringing glamour to the stay-at-home mom? Are you willing to make the investment of the century that will yield gains by one hundred fold? This return is guaranteed to pay off. We welcome you to join us on this journey because it has only begun. We have much to learn, reshape, and refigure now that we are back at home after many decades of the working mother. But that is another book for another time. Until then, stay focused and enjoy every single moment of your motherhood.

References

Miron, Michelle. "More Moms Stepping Out of the Workforce." *Kalamazoo Gazette* 08 05 2005

Warren, Elizabeth & Tyagi, Amelia Warren. *The Two-Income Trap*. New York: Basic Books, 2004.

Stanley, Thomas J., & Danko, William D. . *The Millionaire Next Door*. New York: Pocket Books, 1996.

Orman, Suze. *Nine Steps to Financial Freedom*. New York: Three Rivers Press, 1997.

Orman, Suze. *The Courage to be Rich: Creating a Life of Material and Spiritual Abundance*. New York: Riverhead Books, 1999.

"Freezer Storage Times." *Taste of Home*

Maltby, Tammy & Farah, Tamra. *Lifegiving: Discovering the Secrets to a Beautiful Life*. Chicago: Moody Press, 2004.

U.S. Department of Labor. "Bureau of Labor Statistics." *Mean Hourly Wage*. May, 2004. . June 11, 2005 <bls.gov/oes/oes_dl.htm#2004_m>.

Contact Andrea English and
Elaine Shepherd at
milliondollarmom@mechintel.com

or order more copies of this book at:

TATE PUBLISHING, LLC

127 East Trade Center Terrace
Mustang, Oklahoma 73064

(888) 361 - 9473

TATE PUBLISHING, LLC
www.tatepublishing.com